PRACTICAL HELP FOR NEW SUPERVISORS

THIRD EDITION

Joan Giesecke
Editor

AMERICAN LIBRARY ASSOCIATION
Chicago and London
1997

Project manager: Louise D. Howe

Cover design: Richmond Jones

Text design and composition by Dianne M. Rooney in Sabon and Perpetua using QuarkXpress 3.32 for the Macintosh 7100/66

Printed on 50-pound Victor Offset, a pH-neutral stock, and bound in 10-point C1S Bristol cover stock by Victor Graphics

The paper used in this publication meets the minimum requirements of American National Standard for Information Sciences—Permanence of Paper for Printed Library Materials, ANSI Z39. 48-1992. ∞

Library of Congress Cataloging-in-Publication Data

Practical help for new supervisors / edited by Joan Giesecke for the
    Supervisory Skills Committee, Personnel Administration Section, Library
    Administration and Management Association. — 3rd ed.
        p.   cm.
    Includes bibliographical references.
    ISBN 0-8389-3467-6 (alk. paper)
    1. Library personnel management—United States. 2. Supervision
of employees. I. Giesecke, Joan. II. Library Administration and
Management Association. Personnel Administration Section. Supervisory
Skills Committee.
Z682.2.U5P73   1997
023'.9—dc20   96-35907

Printed in the United States of America.

01 00 99 98 97   5 4 3 2 1

Contents

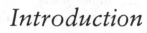

Introduction

Being a supervisor can be a very rewarding experience, but it can also be one of the most difficult things you have ever been asked to do. All too often, new supervisors have had little or no training, and may not even be aware of the skills they lack until a problem occurs. Aimed at the new supervisor, this publication addresses basic supervisory skills and provides practical information needed by supervisors. ·

For this expanded, revised third edition, we have updated the original chapters and have added chapters on managing work time, managing diversity, and conflict resolution. As library organizations become more complex, supervisors must address issues of working in a diverse workplace serving a diverse clientele. In addition, as organizations learn to live with constant change, supervisors may spend more and more time resolving conflicts and helping staff learn to work in a more flexible environment. For this edition, we have addressed these issues that now face all supervisors. As in previous editions, we have included lists of readings for those who seek additional information on these topics.

Special thanks for the completion of this revised edition goes to all members of the LAMA Personnel Administration Section, Supervisory Skills Committee, past and present, who worked many hours to create this publication.

We welcome comments about the usefulness of this publication and suggestions for future topics.

Joan Giesecke
Editor

1

On Becoming a Supervisor

Joan Giesecke

Dean of Libraries
University of Nebraska–Lincoln

It's a big decision! You have been offered a position as a supervisor. Promotion to a supervisory position can be exciting, challenging, and a bit frightening. Your role in the organization is about to change, and you need to think carefully about the advantages and disadvantages of this change. Will you be happy as a supervisor? Are you ready to move into management?

Consider some of the hazards of being a supervisor before you make the change. You will move from being one of the gang to being part of management. Bosses aren't always popular. Are you ready to be part of the group that you and your fellow employees criticized over lunch? Are you ready to appraise the performance of your former colleagues or of your new staff? Are you ready to discipline an employee who is not meeting expectations?

To help you think about being a supervisor, try asking yourself the following questions. Do you prefer working with others to working alone? Do you enjoy teaching others how to do things? Do you enjoy leading others? Do you like to chair meetings? Are you comfortable making decisions? Can you take an unpopular stand on an issue and support it? Are you a good listener? Are you assertive? Can you handle stress? Are you a good planner? If you can answer yes to most of these questions, then you are ready to be a supervisor.[1]

A New Perspective

Once you begin your work as a supervisor, one of the first things you will notice is that you will have a new perspective on the organization. Now, instead of being responsible for completing assigned tasks, you will be responsible for seeing that others complete these tasks. Your major responsibilities will include planning, coordinating the work of your unit, training employees, and ensuring that your unit meets its goals.

The challenge to today's supervisors is to take charge in an environment where supervisors now coordinate the work of others and coach employees rather than controlling the operations. Today's supervisor is expected to be a team leader coordinating group efforts to accomplish organizational objectives rather than a more traditional manager controlling and commanding activities. In addition to technical expertise, today's supervisor needs good communication skills, the ability to delegate effectively, good planning and coordination skills, the ability to manage time effectively, and good decision-making skills. An effective supervisor needs self-confidence, the ability to be flexible and creative, and a sense of humor.

Building Relationships with Your Staff

One of the first tasks for a new supervisor is to build a good working relationship with the members of the unit or department. You can start off on the right foot by always being receptive to your staff. Listen to their ideas and concerns. They may see a situation differently and be able to provide a different perspective on problems. They can help prevent you from making major mistakes in your first few months on the job. During the first few weeks your staff will be making an effort to be cooperative, just as you are learning how to interact with them. Now is the time to learn what your employees think of the unit, what changes they might suggest for improving the operation, and how they do their own jobs. Don't be afraid to ask questions about office routines, policies, procedures, and general organizational folklore. Bluffing your way through is a mistake; you are likely to lose the respect of your staff if they feel you are not interested in learning how the organization functions. Now is not the time to push through your own agenda. Now is the time to listen and learn. Then evaluate how your ideas will mesh with the organization.

It is also important to set a good example. Treat everyone with respect. Remember you need your staff more than they need you. Maintain a regular schedule. Now is not the time to start taking long lunches or not showing up for work. If you do not take your job seriously, why should employees take their jobs seriously?

Building a Relationship with Your Boss

Next you need to build a good working relationship with your boss. Now is the time to find out how your boss prefers to communicate, what objectives management has for your unit, and what part you play in the overall organizational planning structure. Cultivate honest communication with your boss. Open lines of communication are essential if you are to succeed as a supervisor. Ask questions. Relay information to your boss. Be sure your boss knows if a deadline might be missed, or if a problem is developing in your area. Bosses don't need surprises. Keeping your boss informed about your unit will prevent unpleasant surprises that can lead to disasters for you and your unit.

Building Relationships with Your Peers

Now is also the time to begin building a working relationship with a new set of peers, the other supervisors in the organization. At first you may be uncomfortable with this group. As is true anytime you join a new group, you may feel awkward, nervous, jealous, or fearful. These feelings are normal. To become more comfortable working with other supervisors, try getting to know your peers as individuals. Invite another supervisor out to coffee, or to lunch, and begin to build a sense of rapport. Explore the ways your two units are likely to interact, what areas need to be coordinated between the units, and how you can best support each other in the organization. This is a time to listen and learn from your peers as you begin to plan for improving the effectiveness of your unit.

Making Changes Slowly

As a new supervisor you need to resist the temptation to make too many changes too quickly. Take time to get to know the organization and your employees first. Take time to assess the strengths of each member of your staff so you can make informed decisions about the work. Build staff support for proposed changes by involving your staff in the planning process. Learn from their experience in making changes and listen to their cautions about proposed changes. Address their concerns as you move forward with changes. By working together and leading the group, rather than dictating to the group, you can build a unit that works well together and is successful in achieving objectives.

Conclusion

What, then, really changes as you move into a supervisory role? Of course, your job, your responsibilities, and perhaps most importantly, your viewpoint. Initially you may be nervous, anxious, and frustrated. These feelings will lessen as you gain experience, begin making decisions, and develop confidence in yourself. Your sense of isolation will also decrease as you become a part of a new peer group of other supervisors. You will no longer be part of the "old gang," but you will be shaping a new group as you begin to see your unit as a team. By encouraging your staff's participation in the planning for the unit and in making work decisions, you will develop a group of people you can count on to help you help them accomplish their tasks.

Note

1. William Umiker, *Management Skills for the New Health Care Supervisor* (Rockville, Md.: Aspen Publications, 1988), 3–4.

Suggested Reading

Belker, Loren B. *The First-Time Manager.* New York: American Management Association, 1993.

Carr, Clay. *The New Manager's Survival Manual: All the Skills You Need for Success.* 2nd ed. New York: Wiley, 1989.

Everything You Always Wanted to Know about Supervision. Des Moines, Iowa: American Media, 1983. Videotape.

Imundo, Louis V. *Effective Supervisor's Handbook.* New York: American Management Association, 1991.

Pell, Arthur P. *Supervisors Infobank: 1000 Quick Answers to Your Toughest Problems.* New York: McGraw-Hill, 1994.

Stone, Florence, ed. *The AMA Handbook of Supervisory Management.* New York: American Management Association, 1989.

2

Interviewing

Thyra K. Russell

Personnel Librarian
Southern Illinois University at Carbondale

An effective, productive interview can take place only if the interviewer establishes rapport with the candidate through good communication skills and a knowledge of effective interviewing practices.

The employment or selection interview is designed to help the supervisor choose the best applicant for the job, which means making the right hiring choice. During the interview, it is the interviewer's responsibility to obtain from the applicant as much information as possible while describing the job and the library. Both the interviewer and the applicant should use this time to test the personal chemistry—to determine if they can work well with one another.[1] The supervisor knows the duties and responsibilities the position entails and the skills, experiences, and personal qualifications the prospective employee must possess in order to be successful. An interview that has been carefully planned and well conducted should result in the right match for the person, the job, and the library. The purpose of this chapter is to demonstrate how you, as a new supervisor, can achieve this result.

An interview has been described as "essentially a social situation in a business setting."[2] Basic rules of conversation apply. The interview process, however, involves more than just talk and can be divided into three essential parts: preparation, the interview itself, and follow-up.

Before the Interview

Prior to the interview, the supervisor should examine the current job description and review the requirements of the position. The supervisor should also review available materials such as the cover letter, application form, correspondence, resume, test scores, and references of the candidate before the interview takes place. Review the written material for its appearance, legibility, accuracy, and completeness.

Plan how you will conduct your interviews. Make an outline of topics to be covered and things you want to tell the applicants about the work and the library. Think about the types of question that should elicit information necessary to evaluate an applicant, and make a list of general and specific questions. This will ensure that the same key questions are asked of all applicants. In order to adhere to regulations governing equal opportunity, it is also essential to review the kinds of questions that are not permitted under current law.

During the Interview

In order to establish a good rapport and facilitate communication during the interview, the supervisor should:

- Create a welcoming atmosphere by using a private office or meeting room.
- Identify yourself by name and title with a cordial, friendly greeting and firm handshake.
- Determine the applicant's preferred name and repeat it during the interview.
- Start with small talk (if appropriate) to create a relaxed atmosphere.

- Discourage interruptions; give the applicant your full attention.
- Set the agenda by briefly explaining the objectives of the interview.
- Have all the necessary materials available; know the qualities required in order to perform the job well.
- Gather information about the applicant's past; ask questions that allow the applicant to expand upon his or her resume, not just repeat it.
- Maintain eye contact.
- Take appropriate notes without interfering with the smooth flow of the interview; use abbreviations or shorthand.
- Phrase questions to elicit answers beyond a mere "yes" or "no"; use open-ended questions that typically begin with "what," "why," or "how."
- Intersperse direct questions with open-ended questions.
- Ask the same questions of all applicants.
- Focus your attention on the applicant's answers to your questions.
- Do not interrupt the candidate.
- Encourage the candidate to talk freely and spontaneously; don't monopolize the conversation.
- Avoid expressing disagreement or disapproval of a candidate's answers.
- Be aware of nonverbal forms of communication such as body language.
- Be aware of your body position and voice; don't show fatigue, boredom, or lack of interest.
- Maintain objectivity; use common sense and reason; don't allow personal prejudices to affect the interview or hiring decision.
- Use effective listening skills.
- Know how and when to end the interview; allow time for the applicant to ask you questions.
- Anticipate questions the applicant may have about the job, employment benefits, and salary.

- Bring the interview to a close and indicate the time frame within which a hiring decision will be made.

Questions to Avoid

Because of questionable discriminatory hiring practices by some employers in the past, we now have federal, state, and municipal laws that protect employees and job applicants from intentional or unintentional bias by hiring officials. The Equal Employment Opportunity Commission (EEOC) has issued guidelines on questions that may or may not be asked of prospective employees. Certain questions are prohibited by law during an interview or on an application form. These include questions regarding sex, age, race, religion, national origin, or physical condition unrelated to the job qualifications. Two rules govern the Equal Employment Opportunity (EEO) laws and regulations: (1) all questions and qualifications must be job-related; (2) don't ask questions or qualifications of one group (women, racial minorities, disabled, veterans, etc.) that you wouldn't ask the majority group (such as white males).[3] Practically speaking, ask the same questions of all applicants; if in doubt, don't ask.

The following guidelines are based on several federal laws: Title VII of the Civil Rights Act of 1964, the Equal Pay Act of 1963, Age Discrimination in Employment Act of 1967, the Rehabilitation Act of 1973, Vietnam Era Veterans Readjustment Act of 1973, and Executive Orders 11246 and 11375 regarding government contracts. It is unlawful to ask job applicants the following questions:[4]

- Are you married, single, divorced, widowed, etc.?
- What is your age?
- What is your religious denomination or affiliation?
- What is your national origin or ancestry?
- How did you acquire the ability to read, speak, or write a foreign language?
- Are you a member of a particular club, fraternity, or lodge?
- What are your future marital plans?
- Are you pregnant? Do you have children? What are your child care arrangements?

- Will your spouse object to your travel schedule?
- What is the occupation of your spouse, father, sister, etc.?
- What type of discharge did you receive from the military?
- What is your stand on civil rights issues? women's liberation issues?

In other words, if a question is not job-related, don't ask it.

In addition to the laws mentioned above, the 1990 Americans with Disabilities Act prohibits employers from discriminating on the basis of a disability. Questions concerning disabilities cannot be asked on job applications or during interviews. Such questions relate to whether the applicant has been treated or hospitalized for certain conditions or diseases. Specifically, the following questions are illegal:[5]

- Have you ever had or been treated for any of the following conditions or diseases (followed by a checklist of various conditions and diseases)?
- Are there any conditions or diseases for which you have been treated in the past three years?
- Have you ever been hospitalized? If so, for what condition?
- Have you ever been treated by a psychiatrist or psychologist? If so, for what condition?
- Have you ever been treated for any mental condition?
- Is there any health-related reason why you may not be able to perform the job for which you are applying?
- Have you had a major illness in the last five years?
- How many days were you absent from work because of illness last year?
- Do you have any physical defects that prevent you from performing certain kinds of work? If yes, describe these defects and specific work limitations.
- Are you taking any prescribed drugs?
- Have you ever been treated for drug addiction or alcoholism?
- Have you ever filed for workers' compensation insurance?

Questions that *may* be asked of all candidates include the following:[6]

- Can you meet the attendance requirements of this job?
- Can you perform the functions of this job with or without reasonable accommodation?
- Can you describe or demonstrate how you would perform these functions?

A related question that is permissible is "Do you suffer from any physical or mental disabilities that would limit your performance in this job?"[7]

After the Interview

After the interview has been completed, the supervisor should review his or her notes, the applicant's résumé, and samples of work the applicant has provided. Take time to record additional facts or impressions after the interview is concluded. It is important to make notes immediately (within ten minutes) because it may be difficult to remember certain details, especially if several applicants are interviewed in one day.

Finally, after all applicants have been interviewed, it is time to evaluate and compare the education, experience, and ability of the applicants to perform the job. Some supervisors use a rating scale to evaluate and compare applicants, ranking them on their training, ability, experience, interpersonal and communication skills, evidence of leadership, and ability to make decisions.

Next steps may include talking with everyone who participated in the interview process, arranging for a follow-up or second interview, and checking references.

Reference checking usually involves writing or telephoning an applicant's previous employers. Employers often disagree on whether reference checking is useful. Often, references are totally positive or generate minimal information, such as dates of employment and job titles. However, reference checking is a source of information that completes the interview process. Questions asked a previous or present employer should relate to the applicant's work and job performance and include an assessment of the applicant's ability to perform the prospective job.[8]

Information received from references is confidential and should only be discussed with others directly involved in the hiring decision. The interviewer should obtain written permission from the applicant to contact his or her references. It is recommended that the application form contain a statement that gives the interviewer authority to contact former employers in addition to other references supplied by the applicant. This form should be signed and dated by the applicant.[9]

Typical questions the supervisor might ask a reference include the following:[10]

- How would you compare the candidate's performance to that of the person doing the job now? Or: What characteristics will you look for in a replacement?

- If he or she was that good, why didn't you try to induce him or her to stay?

- When there was a particularly urgent assignment, what steps did he or she take to get it done on time?

- Since none of us is perfect, please describe some areas in which he or she could improve.

- Have you seen his or her current résumé? Let me read you the part that describes his or her job with your organization. (Stop at each significant point, and ask the reference for a comment.)

- Not all employees get along well together. What kinds of people did he or she have trouble with?

- How many times a month does he or she arrive late or leave early? On the average, how often does he or she take off for sickness or personal reasons?

- When he or she was hired, were his or her references checked thoroughly? Who checked these references? What did the references have to say?

You may wish to ask other questions of your own, such as: When the applicant says he or she has "finished" a job, is it really finished? Does someone else have to check the applicant's work?

For additional information on the importance of reference checking and ways to avoid potential legal problems, see the books by Robert Wilson and by Richard Rubin listed in the Suggested Reading section.

Conclusion

It is now time to review all material pertinent to each applicant before making a hiring decision. Through good communication and effective planning combined with an awareness of the essential steps in the interview process, the new supervisor should accomplish his or her goal of hiring the "right" person for the job.

Notes

1. James G. Goodale, *The Fine Art of Interviewing* (Englewood Cliffs, N.J.: Prentice-Hall, 1982), 22.
2. Alice Gore King, "How to Interview Job Applicants," *Supervisory Management* 31 (April 1986): 37.
3. Virginia L. Davis, "Selecting the Best Candidate Starts with Good Interviewing Skills," *The CPA Journal* 56 (February 1986): 73–74.
4. Ibid., 72; see sidebar Questions Not to Ask.
5. George D. Webster, "Job Applications, Interviews, and the ADA," *Association Management* 45 (March 1995): 17.
6. William E. Lissy, "Interviewing Job Applicants under the ADA," *Supervision* 56 (March 1995): 17.
7. Richard E. Rubin, *Human Resource Management in Libraries: Theory and Practice* (New York: Neal-Schuman, 1991), 63.
8. Ibid., 76.
9. Ibid.
10. Robert F. Wilson, *Conducting Better Job Interviews* (Hauppauge, N.Y.: Barron's Educational Series, 1991), 46.

Suggested Reading

Buhler, Patricia. "Hiring the Right Person for the Job." *Supervision* 53 (July 1992): 21–23.

Creth, Sheila. "Conducting an Effective Employment Interview." *Journal of Academic Librarianship* 4 (November 1987): 356–60.

Davis, Virginia L. "Selecting the Best Candidate Starts with Good Interviewing Skills." *The CPA Journal* 55 (February 1986): 73–75.

Donaghy, William C. *The Interview: Skills and Applications.* Salem, Wis.: Sheffield, 1990.

Drake, John D. *The Effective Interviewer: A Guide for Managers.* New York: American Management Association, 1989.

Goodale, James G. *The Fine Art of Interviewing.* Englewood Cliffs, N.J.: Prentice-Hall, 1982.

Hequet, Marc. "The Intricacies of Interviewing." *Training* (April 1993): 31–36.

King, Alice Gore. "How to Interview Job Applicants." *Supervisory Management* 31 (April 1986): 37–43.

Lissy, William E. "Interviewing Job Applicants under the ADA." *Supervision* 56 (March 1995): 17–18.

Messmer, Max. "The Art and Science of Conducting a Job Interview." *Business Credit* 97 (February 1995): 35–36.

Rubin, Richard E. *Human Resource Management in Libraries: Theory and Practice.* New York: Neal-Schuman, 1991.

Webster, George D. "Job Applications, Interviews, and the ADA." *Association Management* 45 (March 1993): 154, 157.

Wilson, Robert F. *Conducting Better Job Interviews.* Hauppauge, N.Y.: Barron's Educational Series, 1991.

3

Orienting the
New Library Employee

Katherine Branch

Library Director
Anne Arundel Community College Library

Many supervisors breathe a sigh of relief once they have made a hiring decision. To ensure that the "right candidate" becomes a successful employee, a great deal of time and effort should be devoted to orienting the newcomer. New employees lack a sense of belonging, and this can result in high turnover in the early weeks of employment. The new employee needs to be recognized as a person and feel that the job is important. The first day on the job can influence the way the person feels about the library throughout his or her employment. In addition, an organized plan for orientation that ensures that employees know where to go for help can increase morale and productivity. This chapter will outline how to plan and carry out an orientation program for new library employees. (The chapter does not cover job training.)

Before the Employee Arrives

Find out whether there are standard orientation procedures within the library. If there are not, consider suggesting that procedures be developed. Volunteer to work on a draft of procedures; form a committee to address the issue; or discuss the issue with your personnel librarian. Also, see what your parent institution provides in the way of orientation information. Many universities, government agencies, and corporations provide in-depth orientation sessions or packets.

Preparation for the employee's first day at work is essential. Ask other employees about their orientation experiences and needs. Listen for gaps in their orientation and determine how those gaps affected their performance.

Analyze the job description and specific duties of the new employee. Decide how the employee should be oriented so that she or he has an understanding of how her or his duties fit into the library's mission and relate to the duties of others in the library.

Determine who in the library is best suited to orient the new employee to specific types of information. As the supervisor, you should not do the entire orientation yourself. It is important that the new employee get to know his or her coworkers and their areas of expertise. However, you should retain responsibility for the orientation because you have a vested interest in being sure that the employee is well oriented. In addition, the employee is motivated to learn from you since you will be evaluating his or her performance. Because you want to transmit the codes of conduct important to you, you should not delegate discussions of conduct or behavior to others.

Try to schedule a variety of orientation activities, because people have different methods of learning. Some alternatives to one-on-one discussions include written exercises, workbooks, audiovisual "tours," computer-assisted instruction, small group sessions, and written orientation, policy, and procedure materials.

Determine the time frame for the orientation period based on the job. A part-time shelving job may require a shorter orientation period than a professional reference or cataloging job. When deciding on the length of the orientation period, be sure to allow time for independent exploration by the employee, for formation of on-the-job friendships, and for beginning actual job duties. If new employees do not begin to do some work shortly after their first day, they may feel that they are not making a contribution to the library. They may feel as though others are judging them and wondering why they are not beginning to do "real work." Remember that new employees are anxious and eager to begin work. Capitalize on this enthusiasm!

After completing the orientation plan, you should arrange for the new employee's desk or office space so that it is ready before she or he arrives. A list of supplies is included in the New Employee Orientation Checklist at the end of this chapter.

An essential step in making the new employee feel welcome is to prepare other staff members prior to the new employee's first day. Define the role of the new employee, being clear about the authority and autonomy the new employee will have. This can help prevent unintentional (or intentional) hazing. Hazing can occur when current employees feel threatened by the eagerness and enthusiasm of a new employee. Occasionally a new employee unwittingly encourages hazing by referring to the way things were done in other libraries where she or he worked. Current employees may take such references as a criticism of their library.

Another step is to assign a "buddy" or guide to the new employee—someone from a different department who is friendly and knowledgeable about the library. A staff member from a different department can become a source of information for the new employee about how things are done outside his or her department. Such a guide might undergo training so that she or he knows what is expected in orienting the new employee.

The First Day

The first day is crucial and can have a significant impact on reducing the new employee's anxiety and encouraging a positive attitude. Perhaps the most important aspect of the first day's orientation is becoming aware of and attending to the new employee's social needs.

First, you should tell the new employee how you and others in the library prefer to be addressed. (Be sure the new employee knows how to pronounce difficult names correctly. There is nothing more embarrassing for a new employee than mispronouncing a name!)

Second, she or he should be introduced to her or his coworkers and others with whom she or he will have frequent contact. Schedule time so that the new employee can get to know coworkers. Stress teamwork in your discussions.

Third, the employee should have an introduction to the layout of the building so she or he feels comfortable about being there. Safety and security information should be covered, particularly in a library where theft or personal threats are a potential problem.

Fourth, give the employee a general outline of the job so that she or he is fully aware of, and comfortable with, her or his duties. Provide an orientation packet and discuss particularly important information in the packet.

A first-day orientation might go something like this: The supervisor welcomes the new employee as the new employee arrives and briefly discusses general issues, such as the employee's hours, breaks, conduct, library philosophy, and procedures for reporting absences. The supervisor then introduces the new employee to coworkers. A coworker within the department gives the new employee a tour of the department. Depending on the size of the library, the coworker (or an assigned buddy or guide from another area of the library) gives the new employee a tour of the entire library. Be sure to arrange in advance for the new employee to have lunch with yourself, her or his guide, or a group of coworkers. The library's administrator or personnel librarian should discuss benefits, safety, and grievance procedures. Time should be allowed for the employee to read policies, get accustomed to his or her work area, and think about what has been learned so far.

The First Two Weeks

By the end of the first two weeks, the new employee should be knowledgeable about the functions of other departments within the library and how the employee and his or her department interact with other departments. The new employee should be familiar with the library's organization chart and how the library fits into its parent institution's goals and plans. He or she should know how performance will be evaluated and be aware of acceptable and unacceptable behavior. He or she should know where to go for help and how to contact resource people within the library and institution. Other important topics for the first two weeks are included in the checklist.

The First Month

During the first month, discuss opportunities for advancement and career development with the new employee. By the end of the first month, schedule time for formal feedback about the new employee's orientation period. This meeting will provide an opportunity for you to fill any gaps in the orientation and can help you in planning for the next new employee.

Conclusion

In general, be nonthreatening and observant during the orientation period. Communicate your concerns and be open to the concerns, however trivial sounding, of your new employee. Small concerns, if neglected, can be blown out of proportion. By thoroughly preparing for the orientation period, you can do much to guarantee that your new employee adjusts easily to his or her new environment and becomes a productive employee.

Suggested Reading

Contributed by Melissa Carr, Associate Director, Daniel Boone Regional Library, Columbia, Missouri.

Beeler, Cheryl. "Roll Out the Welcome Wagon: Structuring New Employee Orientations." *Public Management* (August 1994): 13–17.

Berger, Susan. "Ongoing Orientation at Metropolitan Life." *Personnel Journal* (December 1989): 28–35.

Brown, Thomas L. "The Very First Day: An Orientation to the Importance of Orientations." *Industry Week,* no. 240 (June 17, 1991): 19.

Davis, H. Scott. *New Employee Orientation: A How-to-Do-It Manual for Librarians.* New York: Neal-Schuman, 1994.

Markowich, M. Michael, and Jo Anna Farber. "If Your Employees Were the Customers." *Personnel Administrator* (September 1989): 70–73.

Rogers, Shelley L. "Orientation for New Library Employees: A Checklist." *Library Administration & Management* 8 (Fall, 1994): 213–17.

Rubin, Richard. *Hiring Library Employees.* New York: Neal-Schuman, 1993: 107–11.

Wehrenberg, Stephen B. "Skill and Motivation Divide Training and Orientation." *Personnel Journal* (May 1989): 111–13.

World Wide Web Resources

More ideas on orienting new employees can be found on the Internet. To identify current sites, use one of the search engines such as Yahoo, Lycos, WebCrawler, InfoSeek, etc., and search under the terms "employee" and "orientation."

New Employee Orientation Checklist

Before the Employee Arrives

Send a letter to the new employee specifying conditions of employment, such as salary, hours of work, and job title.

Equip the employee's desk or work area with basic supplies:

stapler	paper
cellophane tape	note pads
stationery	staff directory
scissors	phone books
ruler	key procedures manuals
pens, pencils	

Prepare an orientation packet including the following:

- history and philosophy of the library
- organization chart
- descriptions of the functions of each library department
- library staff directory
- library or institution's newsletter
- library's annual report
- map of the institution, campus, or agency
- information on the local area (if the employee is from out of town)

Order a nameplate (pin, badge, etc.) and business cards (check to see how the new employee would like her or his name to appear).

Update the staff directory to include the new employee.

Put the new employee on the mailing list for library and institutional newsletters.

Notify coworkers of the new employee's name, duties, and start date.

Provide the employee with parking information.

→

First Day

Introduce the employee to coworkers.

Conduct a library tour, focusing on rest rooms, cafeteria or lounge, and the location of supplies, photocopy machines, and telephones.

Cover safety and security issues, such as emergency procedures and personal safety.

Discuss hours, breaks, payday, and procedures for reporting absences.

Make lunch arrangements for the new employee with yourself, the new employee's guide, or a group of coworkers.

Tell the employee how you, the coworkers, and the administrators prefer to be addressed (e.g., by your first name, last name, or title).

Discuss the philosophy of the library and its commitment to service.

Discuss standards of conduct and any formal or informal dress code.

Be sure all personnel paperwork is completed.

Second Day

Discuss telephone procedures and policies.

Tour the entire institution or agency, pointing out the credit union, cafeteria, and mail room.

Explain timekeeping procedures, including overtime and compensatory time.

First Week

Review the library's organizational chart and reporting structure.

Arrange for the employee to get ID and library cards.

Explain library policies on such matters as office collections, soliciting, confidentiality of library records, smoking, alcohol, and drugs.

Arrange for an explanation of benefits, such as insurance, vacation, leave policies, retirement, disability, credit union, tuition coverage, holidays, jury duty, bereavement leave, and travel policy.

Explain procedures for communicating problems or concerns.

Cover department-specific plans, policies, and procedures.

Cover housekeeping responsibilities.

Explain the operation of the employee's union (if applicable).

Second Week

Explain any probationary period.

Discuss performance standards and appraisal.

Discuss the library's tenure or salary-review program.

Outline the long-range plans of the library.

Cover grievance procedures.

First Month

Schedule an appointment with the library director and your supervisor.

Arrange for orientation to other departments with which the employee frequently interacts.

Ask for the employee's feedback on the orientation.

Discuss opportunities for advancement.

4

Appraising Performance

Joan Giesecke

Dean of Libraries
University of Nebraska–Lincoln

Appraising performance of employees is one of the most difficult tasks for new supervisors. First-time supervisors are sometimes reluctant to comment on the work of staff members for fear the discussion may ruin the working relationship. Supervisors sometimes inflate ratings to try to keep staff happy, believing that if they can't say something nice, supervisors shouldn't say anything at all. On the other hand, some supervisors may be too harsh, feeling they need to establish themselves as the "boss." Neither strategy will be successful. Rather, appraisals should be an honest evaluation and commentary on how well an employee is doing his or her job.[1]

A good appraisal system is an ongoing process that requires a supervisor to evaluate fairly the tasks the employee performs, and how well the person completes those tasks. The supervisor must be certain that the employee understands how to do the work, knows what the expectations are for completion of the task, and is rewarded for meeting those expectations. By reviewing the work being done on a regular, informal basis, the supervisor can ascertain if the employee is doing a task correctly and can provide guidance more easily if problems develop. Regular reviews will help build trust between the employee and the supervisor. An employee who receives regular feedback on how he or she is doing will not be surprised by any issues raised in a formal evaluation session.

Appraising performance is relatively painless when the employee is doing an outstanding job. The supervisor can provide positive feedback and encouragement, and the appraisal session can become a pleasant conversation. However, sometimes employees are not meeting expectations. Then the supervisor needs to coach and counsel the employee on how tasks need to be accomplished and what will happen if the employee does not meet those expectations. But, before we get to practical help on how to handle the problem cases, let's first review why employees may not be meeting expectations.

Why Employees Don't Meet Expectations

Before deciding how to coach or counsel an employee who is not meeting expectations, the supervisor should examine some of the reasons why an employee may not be carrying out tasks as expected. Are there aspects of the work environment that may be making it difficult for the employee to succeed? Does the employee have the training needed to do the work? Does the person have the resources to do the job? Does the person have the authority to make the decisions needed to complete the assignment? Does the employee know he or she is not meeting expectations? Does the employee believe he or she is doing the work correctly? Does the person think he or she has a better way to carry out the task and is being innovative? Does the person know the priorities for the task assignments or is the person doing a low-priority task thinking it is the one you want done? Do you reward the person for doing things right? Are there any negative consequences for poor performance? Is poor performance tolerated in the organization? Does the person have a reason for changing her or his behavior?

By first examining the context in which the person works, the supervisor can begin to determine what efforts may be needed to motivate the employee to improve his work performance. Unless there is an obvious reason for changing behavior, the person may be reluctant to alter it just because you request a change.

Steps to Improve Work Performance

Supervisors can take a number of steps to improve an employee's work performance.

Orientation and Training

Good work performance starts with a clear understanding between the employee and the supervisor of what is expected and what will happen if those expectations are not met. The process begins with the new employee orientation session. The employee orientation is one of the most important aspects of preventive discipline because this is when the supervisor should lay the groundwork for how work will be appraised. It is the supervisor's responsibility to conduct an orientation program that builds a foundation for a good working relationship by making sure that employees know their duties and responsibilities, and understand the rules and consequences of violating those rules. The orientation sessions also provide an opportunity for employees to raise questions and clarify expectations. By beginning with an open, clear communication process, the supervisor will set the tone for an open working relationship that will encourage employees to take responsibility for their own actions and succeed at their jobs.[2]

Communicating Policy and Procedure Changes

The next step in ensuring good work performance is to communicate changes in rules, policies, and procedures clearly and completely. The supervisor is responsible for communicating changes in organizational rules, policies, or procedures that impact employees' performance. It is not fair to hold an employee accountable for following a change in policy or procedure if that change has not been clearly communicated to the staff. Sending out a written notice of the change may not be sufficient to guarantee that all employees are fully aware of it. Reviewing changes at a department or unit meeting may be more effective because it will allow employees to ask questions about the changes. This way both the supervisor and the employees can be sure they understand the changes, understand why the changes have occurred, and have reviewed how the changes impact the unit.

Identifying Problems

Problems with employee performance should be handled as they occur. Early identification of performance problems and actions taken to correct those problems can postpone or eliminate the need for more serious disciplinary action. Handling problems when they first develop will be less painful than waiting until a problem is too large to be easily solved. Hoping the problem will go away will not help the employee understand where he or she may be failing to meet expectations and will not provide the employee with the feedback needed to improve performance.

In identifying and addressing performance problems, supervisors should:

- Focus on the work by developing a careful definition of the problem, and identifying specific observable and measurable actions.
- Measure the action by identifying assumptions about the situation, and then gathering facts such as how often the problem occurs to test the assumptions.
- Analyze the actions and the facts to determine if the problem can be prevented, if the employee has enough knowledge to carry out the task, or if the assignment is too large for one person to do.
- Develop a plan to improve or maintain the desired action and decide how to let the employee know what the problem is and what will happen if improvement does not occur.
- Meet with the employee to discuss the problem, set a plan of action, and develop a feedback system so the employee can measure changes and improved performance.[3]

By carefully analyzing the situation before meeting with the employee to discuss a performance problem, the supervisor can improve the chances that the problem will be resolved successfully.

Coaching and Counseling Employees on Performance Issues

Coaching and counseling employees on performance issues require careful planning. Supervisors should outline what they will say in the coaching session and what outcomes they will seek in the meeting. In a successful coaching session there will be maximum input from the employee, maximum communication about the changes needed and the consequences of not meeting those expectations, and agreement on how performance will be measured and feedback provided.

In the coaching session the supervisor should include the following five steps:

1. Get agreement from the employee that there is a problem. Supervisors often assume the employee already knows there is a problem and skip the step of clarifying that the problem exists. Yet, in successful coaching sessions, almost half the time will be spent defining the problem and getting agreement that there is a problem that needs to be solved. Supervisors need to be clear about why the change needs to occur. Employees may spend time justifying why they have not been meeting expectations. Supervisors need to guide the conversation until the employee is clear about why the problem is serious and needs to be solved.

2. Once a supervisor has agreement that a problem exists, the conversation can move on to finding possible solutions. The supervisor should encourage the employee to find solutions and suggest changes in behavior to correct the actions. If the supervisor simply tells the employee to change, the employee may have no idea of what to change or how to change.

3. Once alternatives have been discussed, agree upon a solution that both you and the employee can follow. Be sure the

employee is comfortable with the solution, understands how to implement the changes, and agrees to make the changes.

4. Decide how you will follow up on the changes. Plan a follow-up meeting, review how work will be monitored, and agree to a time line for making the changes. Follow-up is crucial or the employee may assume that the requested changes are not all that important and do not have to be implemented. If there are no negative consequences for not changing behavior or no positive rewards for changing, a person is unlikely to make a change in behavior.

5. Recognize any achievement. It is imperative that the supervisor recognize any and all improvements in performance. Otherwise the person may not see any use in making behavior changes.

By following a careful plan of identifying problems, coaching employees, and following up on the changes, supervisors will be more successful in encouraging improved work performance from their employees.[4]

When All Else Fails

Not all employees will respond to coaching and counseling sessions. Sometimes further disciplinary action is needed when employees fail to meet expectations. Discipline is most effective when it is applied in steps. Most processes begin with an oral warning to alert the employee to the problem. If corrective action does not occur, the supervisor issues a written warning, outlining the problem, the steps needed to correct the problem, and the consequences of not meeting expectations. These two steps should be documented. Following the steps can ensure that the supervisor is being clear about expectations and the consequences of not meeting those expectations. If, after an agreed-upon time period, the employee is still not meeting expectations, the supervisor may need to take further action such as suspension of the employee or termination. At this stage, the supervisor should be working with his or her own supervisor, the organization's personnel office, or the human resources department. Most organizations have written guidelines for handling disciplinary procedures that can lead to suspensions or terminations. Be sure to review these guidelines and follow them carefully. Employees will often have a process for appealing disciplinary actions. Supervisors should be sure that they have complete, detailed documentation of what actions they have taken to try to resolve the problem. The documentation may well become the supervisor's defense for any actions the supervisor has taken. By following organizational guidelines, taking positive steps to help employees meet expectations, and documenting steps taken to resolve performance problems, the supervisor will be in a strong position to take any action needed.

Annual Performance Review

Most organizations require an annual written review of each employees's performance. This is an opportunity for the employee and the supervisor to review the past year and to plan goals and objectives for the next year. It is a time for review and reflection. It is not a time for surprises for the employee. If problems are being addressed throughout the year, then the annual review is a time to summarize actions taken, progress made, and plans for continued improvement.

The objectives of a formal performance appraisal are (1) to provide a method for recording unbiased impressions of an employee's performance, (2) to allow for consistency in documenting performance among those conducting evaluations through the use of standard forms, and (3) to provide a method for planning goals and objectives for the next year. The formal appraisal, therefore, should be approached as a means of evaluating employee performance and developing strategies for improving that performance via goal setting.

To complete a successful appraisal interview, a supervisor should carefully prepare for the interview by following these ten steps:[5]

1. Study the position description. Know what the employee should be doing. Check goals and objectives.
2. Evaluate your performance as a supervisor. Have you helped or hindered the employee's performance?

3. Complete the written appraisal using knowledge of past performance, critical incidents, and observations. Do not overemphasize recent events. Consider the employee's performance for the whole year.

4. Prepare for the appraisal interview. What results do you expect from the interview? What contributions has the employee made? Is the employee working up to his or her potential? Does the employee know what is expected? What strengths can you build on? What training or retraining is needed?

5. Schedule the interview. Find a quiet place where there will be no interruptions. Allow plenty of time to discuss performance, goals, and objectives.

6. Review the form with the employee. Listen carefully to the employee's comments. Ask open-ended questions. Keep the conversation job related. Discuss new goals and objectives.

7. Discuss areas for improvement. Develop concrete plans for these areas. Develop a schedule for reviewing objectives and progress in these areas. Be candid and specific in discussing behavior. Include the employee's comments on the form as needed.

8. Close the interview. Summarize major points and goals, objectives, and areas for improvement on which you have agreed. Plan any needed follow-up. End the interview on a positive note. The appraisal is an opportunity to plan for improved performance and to reward successful completion of existing goals and objectives.

9. Sign the appraisal form. After the discussion with the employee, the supervisor and the employee should complete the written appraisal form according to the procedures required by the institution. Remember that the performance appraisal is confidential information. It should be kept in a safe place and should be part of the employee's personnel file.

10. Follow up on the formal appraisal. Training or development programs may result from the interview. Set time frames for measuring performance improvement. Follow the formal review with regular informal reviews to monitor progress on improvements.

Conclusion

Managing and appraising employee performance is an ongoing activity, a part of the routine of being a supervisor and an integral part of the successful supervisor's activities. The Arthur Young *Manager's Handbook* provides a step-by-step review of the elements of a successful appraisal program. As the authors note in the do's and don'ts list, supervisors should do the following:[6]

- Appraise frequently and in a relaxed way in order to avoid the employee's resentment of the formal annual review.
- Talk about strengths and weaknesses objectively. Beware of overreacting to good or bad points.
- Avoid saving praise or criticism for the next appraisal. Try to deal with successes and issues as they arise.
- Provide specific criticism and illustrate the points you are trying to make. Give examples of what should have been done.
- Complete the required appraisal forms carefully. Discuss them with the reviewing manager to get a fuller picture.
- Be open to making changes in job descriptions. They might lead to improved job performance.

A supervisor should *not* do the following:

- Approach difficult appraisals as if the employee were overpaid and unreasonable.
- Believe that simply assessing a bad performance will ensure that an employee will improve.
- Fail to appreciate that team performances are interdependent and complex. A bad or good performance may not lie entirely within the control of any single member.
- Dictate the way employees approach their tasks, unless there is a clear reason to do so. Allow employees to take the initiative whenever possible.
- Obscure criticism by "talking around it." If you do not get to the point, you may fail to get your message across.
- React defensively to complaints about your supervisory style. Instead, listen to what could prove to be valuable feedback.

Performance appraisals are essential to a well-run organization. Supervisors can improve their ability to evaluate employee performance by remembering four simple steps: listen, observe, understand, and discuss. By monitoring performance, being aware of the work of each employee, resolving problems as they arise, and rewarding good performance as it occurs, the supervisor ensures that both supervisor and employee will have a clear understanding of each other's responsibilities for meeting the goals and objectives of the department and the organization.

Notes

1. The Arthur Young *Manager's Handbook* (New York: Crown, 1986), 176.
2. For a detailed account of the progressive discipline process, see Nicole A. Norian and Paul Michaud, *A Continuous Quality Improvement Approach to Discipline* (College and University Personnel Association, 1995).
3. Ibid., 9–10.
4. Ferdinand F. Fournies, *Coaching for Improved Work Performance* (New York: McGraw-Hill, 1987), 195–200.
5. *Human Touch Performance Appraisal* (Des Moines, Iowa: American Media, 1984), videotape.
6. Paraphrased from The Arthur Young *Manager's Handbook,* op. cit., 177.

Suggested Reading

The Arthur Young *Manager's Handbook.* New York: Crown, 1986.

Everything You Always Wanted to Know about Supervision. Des Moines, Iowa: American Media, 1983. Videotape.

Face to Face: Coaching for Improved Work Performance. Hollywood, Calif.: Cally Curtis Company, 1981. Videotape.

Fournies, Ferdinand F. *Coaching for Improved Work Performance.* New York: McGraw-Hill, 1987.

Fournies, Ferdinand F. *Why Employees Don't Do What They Are Supposed to Do and What to Do about It.* New York: McGraw- Hill, 1988.

Goodale, James G. *One to One: Interviewing, Selecting, Appraising, and Counseling Employees.* New Jersey: Prentice-Hall, 1992.

Human Touch Performance Appraisal. Des Moines, Iowa: American Media, 1984. Videotape.

Norian, Nicole, and Paul Michaud. *A Continuous Quality Improvement Approach to Discipline.* Washington, D.C.: College and University Personnel Association, 1995.

Sachs, Randi Toler. *Productive Performance Appraisals.* New York: American Management Association, 1992.

Swan, William S., and Phillip Margulies. *How to Do a Superior Performance Appraisal.* New York: Wiley, 1991.

5

Rewarding Employees Nonmonetarily

Irene M. Padilla

Director, Harford County Library, Maryland

and

Thomas H. Patterson

Allentown, Pennsylvania

Library managers must think creatively when deciding how to reward employees. Often budgets are decided by politicians, administrators, or citizens far removed from the realities of maintaining a viable library system. Supervisors may have little control over how salary money is distributed. Labor contracts or other institutional agreements may further limit options. Staff may receive a yearly cost-of-living raise or perhaps some type of merit increase. Compensation of this nature, however, may not ensure that employees find satisfaction and fulfillment in their work. It is important to be aware of the ways in which nonmonetary incentives can be used to supplement the more traditional reward structure offered in your library systems.

Advantages and Disadvantages of Nonmonetary Rewards

Nonmonetary rewards can intensify the employees' desire to succeed and can promote employee self-esteem. They compensate for the supervisor's frequent inability to dispense money or more conventional rewards. This is especially true in public-sector organizations such as libraries. Nonfinancial incentives can offer greater autonomy, job variety, enhanced opportunity for expression and creativity, and the opportunity to develop greater self-respect.

It must also be recognized that a failure to provide nonmonetary rewards carries some built-in hazards that wise supervisors will avoid. First, library managers may well be at a competitive disadvantage if they ignore the value of these benefits. Supervisors who regularly employ nonmonetary incentives may end up outperforming units that discount them. Second, employees working in units where nonmonetary rewards are unavailable may become discontent when they perceive the benefits being provided elsewhere within the same organization.

Jealousy or double-standard situations within a unit are real dangers and must be kept in mind. Employees who do not benefit from nonmonetary rewards may not know why, and they may resent their more privileged colleagues. At times supervisors may purposely or inadvertently tolerate some idiosyncratic behavior (e.g., somewhat inappropriate dress, lack of punctuality, and so on) in certain valued employees that they would not accept from less productive or marginal staff members. Although this approach does have validity, if it is not carefully controlled it can result in charges of favoritism.

It should also be pointed out that there are situations in which management's freedom to utilize nonfinancial incentives may be severely limited. Rigid state personnel regulations, institutional policies, and collective bargaining agreements can seriously restrict a supervisor's ability to think creatively.

Types of Nonmonetary Rewards

Nonmonetary incentives fall into a variety of categories, some of which may be more appropriate than others in your particular setting.

Flexible Scheduling

Flexible scheduling has many variations including flextime, flexitour, flexiplace, variable day, variable week, and so on. All give employees the freedom to plan work schedules around other important factors in their lives. This approach helps them fulfill several roles in their lives without sacrificing one or more for others. An employee's ability to schedule his or her job can be extremely rewarding and may help to improve the quality and quantity of work produced. While many library systems are beginning to feel that this type of scheduling should be routinely offered to all employees, it continues to be thought of as a reward in many libraries. Because most libraries are open far more than forty hours a week, flexible scheduling offers mutually satisfying arrangements for both management and staff.

Flextime denotes a variety of arrangements employees may adopt to complete their assigned number of work hours. A subcategory is *flexitour,* which allows employees to determine the time they leave by the time they started. It requires employees to put in a specified number of hours each day but affords them the flexibility of deciding when they will begin and end the day. *Flexiplace* allows an employee to decide where she or he will most efficiently and effectively accomplish a particular day's work. For example, employees may decide that they will accomplish more at home if they are working on a project that requires attention to detail with a minimum of interruptions. *Variable day* permits employees the opportunity of varying the length of time worked each day as long as they complete the required number of hours each week or pay period. A *variable week* allows employees to decide how many hours they will work each week, with limits placed on the minimum and maximum number of hours or days that must be worked each week or pay period.[1]

Job Design

Job design consists of two components: job enrichment and job rotation. Job design allows employees to learn new skills while keeping their current positions in the organization.

Job enrichment is described as providing "a more holistic approach toward job design and redesign. This is an effort to provide more challenge to employees by adding more tasks and/or more responsibilities to their position."[2] It can be especially valuable in dealing with employees who have reached a plateau in their current positions. This technique can also "encourage the acceptance of responsibility at the bottom of the organization."[3]

An employee who has clearly mastered basic job responsibilities and has energy and time to spare may be permitted the freedom to pursue projects of special interest, even if these activities are not an integral part of her or his job description.

According to Dennis Dresang, job rotation offers another way

> to provide for more diversification, creativity, and challenge. The match between jobs and employees, in these situations [should be] such that employees can replace one another without any noticeable loss in expertise. By periodically rotating individuals to different positions, managers keep morale and productivity at higher levels.[4]

He goes on to caution that both job enrichment and job rotation are

> based on the assumption that work itself is important to employees and that employees are motivated by the nature of their work. . . . This assumption is not warranted for all employees. Because of the limits to the general approach of motivating employees by adding to their tasks and responsibilities and because of the additional constraints provided by unions and classification systems, job rotation and job enrichment have had few applications in the public sector.[5]

Hoopla

In their book *In Search of Excellence,* Thomas Peters and Robert Waterman discuss the motivating power of "hoopla."[6] This process encourages employees to celebrate accomplishments, such as the completion of various phases of a project, or the fact that the employees were selected to perform a special project for the organization. It encourages employees to feel that the organization values their participation because their accomplishments merit attention from management, thus improving morale. It also encourages employees to develop a sense of esprit de corps. Other examples of hoopla might include setting aside a special day, or portion thereof, to allow staff to get together to share food, ideas, and each other's company; posting a visible chart that keeps staff apprised of the accomplishments of their unit compared to the previous month or the previous year; encouraging committees and task forces to adopt a special name that will reflect the group's extra effort and lend an element of prestige to their project.

Day-to-Day Rewards

There are also many simple, less involved ways by which a supervisor can reward employees nonmonetarily. Respect can be demonstrated by sharing time, seeking and giving ideas, listening, advising, and providing general support and encouragement. Staff members may be pleased by desirable committee appointments or related assignments either within or outside the library. Appointments or nominations of this type express confidence in an individual and can aid significantly in career development. Many trusted assistants would be flattered and gratified if asked to represent their organization at professional functions or accompany their supervisor to appropriate business meetings. A supervisor could also acknowledge and utilize an employee's expertise by extending an invitation to coauthor a publication or work jointly on a special initiative.

A competent employee has every right to expect significant responsibilities to be delegated to his or her purview. Delegation gives an employee the opportunity to learn new techniques or hone existing skills. It is important to remember that delegated responsibilities must be accompanied by the authority to carry them out.

In some instances, trusted senior employees in the midst of severe but temporary personal problems, such as divorce or a family death, may be granted more leeway than a strict reading of the personnel manual would imply.

Employees who are consistent producers should be provided with all of the supplies, equipment, space, and staff required to meet their responsibilities. A corollary holds that staff members who are less productive or cooperative should not be supported as generously.

Other Rewards

A conscientious supervisor will energetically pursue organizational perks on behalf of worthy staff members. Such rewards may include emeritus status, service pins, plaques, tuition waivers or reimbursement, nominations for special awards, support for leave of absence or sabbatical, and time for professional travel or related activities. Written letters of appreciation, comments in annual reports, oral recognition, and praise before others, such as the employee's peers and your own supervisors, should not be forgotten.[7] Appropriate written and spoken comments made as part of the regular, formal evaluation process are an important, though often overlooked, source of recognition.

Conclusion

A manager must always keep in mind the ultimate goal of any reward system. For nonmonetary rewards to prove effective, the supervisor must first assess the existing situation and the benefits to both employees and management of introducing these rewards. This will help determine which rewards are most appropriate and assist in the selection of those that best fit the organization's policies and procedures.

Notes

1. Dennis L. Dresang, *Public Personnel Management and Public Policy* (Boston: Little, Brown, 1984), 146.
2. Ibid., 144.
3. Richard J. Stillman, *Public Administration: Cases and Concepts* (Boston: Houghton Mifflin, 1983), 336.
4. Dresang, *Public Personnel Management*, 144.
5. Ibid.
6. Thomas J. Peters and Robert H. Waterman, Jr., *In Search of Excellence: Lessons from America's Best-Run Companies* (New York: Harper and Row, 1982), 58.
7. Michael LeBoefu, *Getting Results: The Secret to Motivating Yourself and Others* (New York: Berkeley Books, 1989), 97–108.

Suggested Reading

Contributed by Adam Szczepaniak, Director of Library Services, Dakkro, Inc., Edgewood, Maryland.

Anderson, A. J., ed. How Do You Manage? (Column). *Library Journal.*

Boyle, Daniel C. *Secrets of a Successful Employee Recognition System.* Portland, Ore.: Productivity Press, 1995.

Deeprose, Donna. *How to Recognize and Reward Employees.* New York: AMACOM, American Management Association, 1994.

Hale, Roger L. *Recognition Redefined: Building Self-Esteem at Work.* Exeter, N.H.: Monochrome Press, 1993.

Harrington, H. James. *Total Improvement Management: The Next Generation in Performance Improvement.* New York: McGraw-Hill, 1995.

Hill, Linda A. *Becoming a Manager: Mastery of a New Identity.* Boston: Harvard Business School Press, 1992.

Klubnik, Joan P. *Rewarding and Recognizing Employees: Ideas for Individuals, Teams and Managers.* Chicago: Irwin Professional Publications, 1995.

Nelson, Bob. *1001 Ways to Reward Employees.* New York: Workman Publications, 1994.

Peters, Thomas J., and Robert H. Waterman, Jr. *In Search of Excellence: Lessons from America's Best-Run Companies.* New York: Harper and Row, 1982.

Pitts, Colin. *Motivating Your Organization: Achieving Business Success through Reward and Recognition.* New York: McGraw-Hill, 1995.

Wilson, Thomas B. *Innovative Reward Systems for the Changing Workplace.* New York: McGraw-Hill, 1995.

Checklist of Nonmonetary Rewards

Flexible scheduling (flextime, flexitour, flexiplace, variable day, variable week, and so on)—giving employees the freedom to plan work schedules around other important factors in their lives.

Job design (job rotation and job enrichment or enlargement)—motivating employees by expanding their tasks and responsibilities.

Hoopla—celebrating milestones on the job to improve morale.

Sharing time with the employee.

Seeking and giving ideas.

Listening.

Advising.

Providing general support and encouragement.

Providing desirable committee appointments or related assignments.

Asking the employee to represent the library at professional functions.

Asking the employee to accompany you to appropriate business meetings.

Extending an invitation to coauthor a publication or work jointly on a special initiative.

Delegating responsibilities with authority to carry them out.

Allowing freedom to pursue projects of special interest.

Other rewards:
- Emeritus status
- Service pins
- Plaques
- Tuition waivers or reimbursement
- Nominations for special awards
- Support for a leave of absence or sabbatical
- Time for professional travel or related reports
- Oral recognition
- Praise before others, such as the employee's peers or your own supervisors

6

Communication Skills

Abby Kratz

Special Assistant to the Provost, University of Texas, Dallas

and

Melinda Flannery

Head of Cataloging, Rice University

H ow effectively do you communicate with others? Do you express your ideas clearly? Are you reasonably certain that you make your point when you write a memo, converse with a colleague, or make a presentation? Conversely, do you listen to, read, and respond to others the way you would like them to respond to you?

Your communication skills are the key to your success as a supervisor. Whether the organization is small and has only a few levels, or very large with multiple levels of hierarchy, the supervisor always occupies a position somewhere in the middle of the organizational chart and must communicate effectively in several directions to function optimally in the organization.

For the new supervisor in particular, communication is a critical element. In the first days and weeks of a new position, no aspect of management is more important to the supervisor than communication. After all, on the first day the new supervisor may know about the organization only as much as she was able to glean in the interview and subsequent negotiations. Additionally, she may know neither where to park nor how to get photocopies made. Part of any new position involves getting the lay of the land, finding out how to get things done, and becoming acquainted with the group of people through whom that particular organization functions.

Communication Channels

A good supervisor will make it a priority to communicate well with her own supervisor. Only thus will she know what the organization expects her to do with the resources she has been given and how her success will be measured. In the first days of a new position, the observant supervisor will note her boss's communication patterns and style. There may be a very formal orientation or training program in which the boss and other key people spend significant amounts of time with the new supervisor, guiding her in developing technical skills, background knowledge, and a sense of how the organization works. In other settings, the boss may be able to spend very little time with the new supervisor, and may seem not to have prepared for much orientation or training. The new supervisor will have to take cues from the boss on these matters. She will learn what level of communication the boss considers to be a good use of his or her time, and what methods are most effective in getting needed answers or direction. She also will learn when the boss expects matters to be treated as confidential and when she is expected to keep her staff informed. She will learn how receptive her boss is to hearing about problems and will find effective ways of gaining support when support is critical.

The effective supervisor also will communicate well with staff members who report to her. She will know what the staff need to do their work, and she will do her best to get the needed resources. These resources may be anything from equipment repair to improved climate control, from training in new skills to improved documentation. It is very important to establish a relationship of openness, honesty, and support, so that staff consider it worth their while to contribute ideas and suggestions and to report problems. Open staff meetings and informal conversations are often used in the relatively intimate circle of a work group. Within the first few weeks, it can be helpful to ask each staff member to sign up for a private conference with the new supervisor, so that she can establish a rapport and round out her orientation. The supervisor might ask questions such as: "What do you do? What do you think works well here? Is there anything you think could be improved? What do you expect of me?" Asking for input, then using it, will encourage staff to continue to communicate honestly with the new supervisor in the future.

The new supervisor also will need to serve as a conduit for information she gets from her boss or from other groups with which she may be involved. A front-line supervisor will often be in the position of communicating a decision that has already been made by others. She should communicate such decisions clearly and with all the understanding she can provide, and involve the staff in the details of implementation whenever possible. Somewhat less often the supervisor will be given complete responsibility for designing a response or solution to a problem. She will have to decide how much staff input is appropriate to the situation, and find effective ways of obtaining it and other information so that the most workable solution is reached.

A less obvious but very important communication channel used by the new supervisor will be communication with peers. A peer is in a more neutral hierarchical position in relation to the new supervisor than the boss or the staff, and therefore may be a good choice for a lunch partner. Getting to know peers can give the new supervisor valuable informal information about the organization as well as establish relationships that may strengthen cooperation in future group projects or committee work. While maintaining appropriate discretion and a professional attitude, the new supervisor may from time to time ask peers to act as sounding boards or provide reality checks on complex situations.

Every organization has a grapevine, and the new supervisor should be aware of it and its contents. The grapevine can be a good source of data about which issues are important, though the information about the issues is often unreliable. For example, while the rumors about a hiring freeze may be false, the concern over workload and job security will remain very real. If staff learn to trust the new supervisor, they will sometimes approach her with reports from the grapevine and ask for verification or denial of rumors and other reports. The supervisor cannot always share all information, particularly information about early planning for sensitive projects or that concerning personnel matters. However, staff should have access to as much reliable information from the supervisor as possible so that they do not have to depend on the often inaccurate information on the grapevine. If the supervisor does not have the information, she should get as much as she can. If the confidentiality of information is unclear, the new supervisor should ask.

Every organization constitutes a unique context in which communication takes place. The new supervisor must observe what kinds of communication are supported in the new environment, and take advantage of them. Communication tends to be less formal in small organizations than in large ones. Communication is affected greatly by the availability of tools such as the telephone, the personal computer, electronic mail, the photocopier, and the fax machine. Certain tools may be available in the organization, yet not very convenient for the new supervisor. For example, electronic mail may be an effective way of communicating some kinds of information to staff. However, if even one staff member does not have access to electronic mail, the communication tool will seem divisive and may suffer in effectiveness. Certain contact people may respond best to telephone calls, yet the new supervisor may not have a telephone on her desk. Indeed, her new desk may be in an office setting where privacy for meetings must be sought elsewhere.

The Communication Process

The basic elements of the communication process remain constant regardless of the physical or organizational context in which the new supervisor must function, and effective communication starts with an understanding of the process by which we send and receive messages.

The first principle to remember is that communication is a system. It takes at least two people for communication to occur: someone to send a message and someone to interpret it. Just as a word has no meaning until it is used in a sentence, a message has no significance until someone receives and interprets it. Like any systemic activity, communication creates a situation of shared responsibility. If the message fails to get through, it is rarely the complete fault of only one of the people involved.

Every communication begins in the mind of an individual. A person who sends a message has something to express, and has at her disposal numerous means of expression. She can write or speak. When she writes, she can use graphics or different fonts to make her point. When she speaks, she can vary her tone of voice by shouting or whispering and use gestures, from grand to minimal. The wise supervisor will think before she puts her thoughts into words, carefully weighing the advantages of spoken or written communication to accomplish the task at hand.

Once an individual has decided what to say and how to say it, it is important to take care to minimize "noise" that might interfere with the clear passage of the message from the originator to the receiver. In written communication, noise can appear as anything from an egregious error in grammar to poor spelling or pale printing. In oral communication, noise can be competing sound in the environment, or it might be an annoying mannerism like a nervous laugh or putting your hand in front of your mouth when you speak. Since communication skills play a major role in the new supervisor's success, it is wise always to look for evidence of such "noise," something that might make it difficult for others to focus on the message.

The second principle of communication to keep in mind is the fact that it is an ongoing process that both includes and transcends the specific messages we intend to send. We are always sending an array of messages. The clothes we are wearing, the way we stand, the way we sit: all are transmitting a message that someone is going to interpret. Don't limit your evaluation of your communication effectiveness to words, spoken or written. What message does your posture give? Your tone of voice? The way you dress? Be aware of your personal style and the messages it transmits.

Conversely, we are always trying to find meaning in everything that the people around us say and do, or don't say and don't do. It remains a good idea for any supervisor to develop her skills at reading the obvious and not-so-obvious messages that are swirling around her.

The third principle of communication is this: we have no control over the interpretation that the audience is going to make. The best we can do is make the message we want them to receive as clear as possible. If we make a habit of communicating candidly and fairly, however, we can improve the probability that our readers and listeners will respond positively to our attempts at communication. We can model the way we want others to interpret what we say and write by responding positively to their attempts at communication.

Writing

With these general principles in mind, let's turn to that ubiquitous form of written communication, the memorandum. Whether transmitted through the organizational mail system, dispatched on the local LAN, or simply pinned onto the area bulletin board, memos probably constitute the most common method for moving information through an organization. Clear and effective memo writing is a skill well worth mastering both for the command it gives the new supervisor over a task that must be repeated constantly and because the principles of producing a good memo apply to all the other modes of communication that a supervisor is expected to employ. Think about it: everybody receives dozens of memos a week. Wouldn't you rather read a well-written one? And wouldn't you be likely to develop a positive attitude toward its writer?

Before sending your next memo, stop to think in advance of the most and least positive outcomes. Whenever you can, identify your purpose and the desired outcome specifically and clearly. If you can't state your goal, how can you reach it? Imagine that your purpose is not just to announce a meeting to discuss an important new policy but also to promote interest in that meeting. You don't want anyone to ignore your message. You probably don't want anyone to be confused or outraged by it either. On the positive side, you would like your staff to understand the intent of the meeting and perhaps the nature of the policy to be discussed. You would like them to look forward to the meeting and begin to prepare for it.

Now design the memo, working back from this desired outcome. It might even help to draft a bad memo in order to remind yourself of the elements of an effective one. A well-designed memo makes use of the three impact points that appear in any communication: the opening, the body, and the conclusion.

The Opening

The first impact point is your opening. A good memo immediately grabs the reader's attention. What is the first thing your reader will notice? Chances are it is the subject heading. Avoid vagueness. If the subject is a change in the fee charged for overdue books, don't say the subject is "Fines Policy." When you have control over the fonts and spacing, you can switch the font to script or bold on the subject line or make some other unexpected visual alteration of the heading and introductory parts of the memo to help seize the attention of your reader.

Equally important in attracting attention is the first sentence of the memo itself. Remember, your reader is busy, so get to the point. Your first sentence should build on the assumption that the reader did read the subject heading. Don't repeat or forget that heading, but rather build on it. Assume that the heading identified your subject as "Possible Increase in Late Fees." Make the first sentence expand and continue the idea mentioned in that heading.

The Body of the Memo

The second impact point is the overall form of the memo. Does this design reflect your control over the material and your appreciation for your audience? Now that you have their attention, you owe them a message that clearly reflects your purpose. Good professional writing should aim at the "three Cs of excellence": consistency, coherence, and clarity.

Whatever you write should reflect a consistent vision and be expressed in a consistent voice. The tone should not veer without warning from formal to chatty. If you are writing a formal proposal, cite evidence that supports your suggestion. Since the reader should not have to figure out just what your main point is, you should not introduce information that does not pertain to it. An old formula for good business writing breaks down the process into three straightforward parts: state what you plan to say, say it, then remind your reader that you said it.

This aspect of consistency leads naturally to the value of coherence. Each paragraph should relate to the previous one and build toward the next. Don't pad anything you write—not your memos, not your proposals, not your résumé. For the intelligent reader, padding qualifies as a form of noise; it is annoying because it implies that the reader cannot distinguish important from peripheral information.

What does your potential audience value? When the answer is "accuracy," offer specific details. Most people who are reading professional material are in a hurry. They want the information or the argument presented clearly and succinctly. Write with those readers in mind.

This basic principle holds equally true whether you are framing an argument to influence your peers, your subordinates, or those above you on the hierarchy. Since you aren't trying to convince yourself, compose your argument for your audience. Professionals want to be persuaded, not manipulated. They will respond more favorably to a presentation that speaks to their intelligence.

The final principle, clarity, should remain in your mind as you compose each sentence. Like padding, excessive rhetoric will cloud the emerging message. Sentences filled with circumlocution, unusual manifestations of vocabulary virtuosity and complex grammatical structures tend to interest the writer far more than the typical business reader.

The Conclusion

The third and final impact point is your conclusion. A strong message ends with a bang rather than just fading away. Good documents, like good presentations, end with a summary and/or a reminder of the main point that has been expressed. If you cannot articulate the main point in a final paragraph, then think again about sending that document.

Speaking and Presenting

Perhaps even more than written communication, oral communication pervades every level of the organization. From the casual greetings staff exchange when they arrive at work to the most formal meeting of an operational or working group, talking is at the heart of work and of supervision. As a new supervisor, you will be called upon to speak in a number of work situations including making presentations to groups, working within groups, and in various one-on-one settings with individuals. Important verbal interaction will occur with staff, with peers, and with your bosses, both in clearly work-related contexts and in informal exchanges.

Many of the steps in preparing a formal presentation for a group will echo those basic to preparation of the memo: define the desired result; get the attention of your audience; eliminate as much extraneous noise from the presentation environment as you can; make your argument or summary clear, concise, and convincing. However, the immediate presence of the audience, the "receiving" end of the system of communication, adds an important dimension to this mode of communication.

Begin to prepare your presentation by defining the desired result. Your purpose in making this presentation might be simply to inform, or it might be to persuade the audience to support an initiative or a solution to a problem. In many cases, an informative presentation may also offer some opportunity to persuade. If you have an opinion of which you wish to persuade others, you will want to be prepared to persuade if the opportunity arises.

Getting the attention of the audience starts with the setup of the room and the behavior and appearance of the speaker. The speaker is often not in control of the room setup, but should be aware of its effect. If you are expected to speak from a chair at a conference table, the atmosphere is more intimate than if you are expected to climb to a podium in front of an audience seated in rows of chairs. A large room creates more distance and formality than a smaller one. Use your understanding of the physical options available to decide how best to hold the attention of the audience. You can decide to sit or stand, use a podium or ignore it, select a particular seat at the table. Sitting at the head of the table is generally the privilege of the group leader or convener.

Choosing a spot that maximizes visibility will increase the chance that the presentation is easily seen, but care also should be taken that the presentation can be well heard. The speaker's appearance should be neat and appropriate to the organizational context.

Informational presentations should provide sufficient background so that the specific topic can be properly understood by the given audience. The new supervisor cannot assume that the audience has her detailed knowledge of the subject under discussion. For example, if the supervisor is asked to present the production statistics of the copy cataloging operation, she should use technical terms such as "volumes" and "titles cataloged" clearly and distinctly. On the other hand, the background and level of the audience must be considered when deciding what level of detail to use. The Director's Advisory Council will not want as much detail, or as long a presentation, on such a topic as will the Technical Services Department. It can be helpful to ask the person who arranges or requests the presentation how long it should be.

Additionally, it is important to be aware of any mental agenda of the audience. You may need to relate the statistics to those of other years or other operations and be prepared to explain why the trend is going up or down. Again, the person who invited you to speak may be of help. Depending on the organization and its formality, the audience may appreciate a written handout of the main points. Judicious use of neat, well-formatted visual illustrations, such as charts or graphs, may help to get more complex information across. Welcome questions—they show you have stirred some thought—and be prepared with answers to those you can anticipate for the meeting and promises you will fulfill to deliver other answers as soon as possible after the meeting.

When asked to make a persuasive presentation to a group, be careful to gather all supporting points for your position and to present them in an orderly, logical manner. Information to back up the points should be included in the presentation only in the volume appropriate to the audience, but should be available for use as needed during questioning.

Additionally, it is useful to rehearse, at least mentally, objections to your points so that questions can be fielded gracefully. If there are obvious apparent objections to your position, consider including the objections and your answers to them in the presentation itself. Sometimes, it may be appropriate to speak informally with some members of the expected audience beforehand, in order to tailor the presentation more effectively to their concerns and make persuasion more likely.

When the new supervisor's role in a group is as a participant or member, rather than as a presenter, the purposes of her oral participation can be more varied, even within a single meeting. She can share reactions to common organizational experience, inform others regarding developments in her area, influence decisions, and simply learn from the participation of others. A supervisor who is new to an organization will do well to take cues from others, especially the leader, about how to participate in the group. A period of orientation is appropriate in every group situation. Some helpful guidelines might be to speak only when you have something to contribute, speak succinctly, be wary of monopolizing the group by speaking too long, but make an effort to contribute to the group both for the good of the group's purpose and to show you can be an asset to future group efforts. A new supervisor is more likely to be asked to be a group member than to lead a group. This provides an excellent opportunity to observe how the chair leads the group and to begin assessing what seems to be effective and what you might want to do differently.

Everyday Communication

Oral communication with individuals can include a broad range of human contact and physical settings. In some situations, the new supervisor may not have a private office, but sensitive conversations with staff should always be conducted in a private area. It will be your responsibility to locate an appropriate space, whether it is an available office, a conference room, or even a brief moment in a private carrel. Many more informal opportunities for conversation will occur in such places as the staff lounge, at the photocopier or the fax machine, and in the parking lot. Even if the contexts are informal, the new supervisor should know that the broader context is always work-related, conduct herself in a professional manner, and not be surprised when work matters come up and sometimes receive substantial discussion. Particularly if the work space is open, the new supervisor should be sensitive to the impact of even work-related conversation on the concentration of other nearby staff members.

Recognition and praise are important to everyone, and the new supervisor should not neglect this kind of communication. She will know from her own experience that most people are motivated by appreciation. However, not every supervisor is comfortable with all forms of recognition, and staff members may prefer to be recognized one way rather than another. When lauding performance or a special accomplishment, it is important to be specific; generality might cast suspicion on the sincerity of the praise. The new supervisor should notice what methods of praising seem to be most effective with her staff. A private word or a brief note of praise can carry a sincere message of appreciation. Significant accomplishments should occasion a letter for the employee's personnel file. Some staff members appreciate being recognized in front of others, but some do not. Choosing methods the supervisor can use naturally and comfortably will increase the sincerity and effectiveness of the praise.

Social situations at work sometimes require a delicate balance from the new supervisor. Every workplace will have different norms from recognizing birthdays, showers, and holidays to who goes to lunch with whom and whether people socialize after work. Use of work time for parties varies by institution; the boss should be consulted if this point is unclear. Particularly within her own staff, the supervisor has a responsibility to treat everyone fairly and recognize everyone equally. Occasional social activities that involve the whole work group may well be normal and accepted. Socializing on an individual basis is probably better done with peers than with selected members of the staff.

Special Situations

As a supervisor, eventually you will find yourself in communication situations in which you are counseling a subordinate or coaching a peer. The basic principles of communication apply in these conversations. You are still involved as part of a system: the other person is just as important to the success of the meeting as you are.

Counseling, however, calls for heightened and slightly differ-ent listening skills. It is imperative that you make certain that the other person is hearing the message that you intend. It will be use-ful to ask at regular intervals for him to rephrase or repeat the message you are sending. If his understanding seems inconsistent with your intent, it is important to take the time to restate your message. In such situations, the other person often is nervous and therefore particularly susceptible to distractions. It is essential to minimize any possible noise. The supervisor should arrange before the meeting to put all telephone calls on hold or have them for-warded. If someone tries to interrupt, politely but firmly send that individual away. With experience the new supervisor will learn how easy it is to "lose" someone in this situation. A simple act such as looking at your watch or breaking eye contact to glance out the window can destroy trust and cost you the opportunity to help solve a problem.

Supervisors inevitably deal with complaints and expressions of dissatisfaction. Responding to a concerned or distraught sub-ordinate requires a different form of communication—empathic rather than analytical. In this case, emotions are not an obstacle to understanding the message, the emotions *are* the message. Your goal, therefore, is to imagine and understand the other person's point of view. You may disagree with it or find his reasons for unhappiness unconvincing, but emotions are often more powerful than reason. You cannot deal together with the causes of the emo-tional distress until you have calmed the other person and gained his appreciation of your willingness to hear his side.

Empathic communication has four intertwined purposes. You will not necessarily accomplish them in the order given here, but an effective supervisor will keep all four in mind as she listens and speaks:

1. Affirm the legitimacy of the other's feelings.
2. Understand the situation or problem from the other's perspec-tive.
3. Endorse the importance of both the speaker and the issue.
4. Empower the speaker to find a resolution to the problem.

The supervisor is not a professional therapist and should not be tempted to help a good employee solve personal problems. The goal in empathic listening is to assist your staff member in removing obstacles to successful work performance.

To create an affirming environment, give the other person your undivided attention. Move from behind your desk (a seating arrangement that emphasizes your control). As the other person talks, avoid the temptation to suggest an immediate solution or to compare the other's troubles to your own. Limit your responses to questions seeking clarification or restatements of what you are hearing. By restating in your own words the other person's description of a situation you are both making sure of your understanding and assuring him that you are paying close attention.

Finally, as a supervisor you want to encourage the commitment, competence, and creativity of your subordinates. Listen and respond empathetically to their expressions of excitement and their new ideas as well as their statements of dissatisfaction and worry. When a subordinate brings a new idea, the supervisor should respond to the excitement in a positive way. Ask clarifying questions while holding off on possible difficulties. The time will come to deal with the problems inherent in any suggestions. If you bring up your objections too quickly, others will stop coming to you with new ideas, and you may lose the opportunity to improve the library and the careers of your subordinates.

Conclusion

In your career as a supervisor you will have many opportunities to hone your skills as a communicator. This short guide should provide you with insight into the processes and help you sidestep some of the pitfalls. Remember that good communication always requires thoughtful preparation. The new supervisor should think carefully about the goal of each situation, choose an appropriate time, and select an appropriate method available to communicate effectively. Carefully planned and executed formal presentations and reports will enhance your image as a leader, and thinking carefully before you telephone, write a memo, or e-mail your boss will help you to establish a reputation as a solid professional who knows what to do to get the job done.

Suggested Reading

Alessandra, Tony, and Phil Hunsaker. *Communicating at Work.* New York: Simon & Schuster, 1993.

Kaumeyer, Richard A., Jr. *How to Write and Speak in Business.* New York: Van Nostrand Reinhold, 1985.

Kratz, Dennis M., and Abby Robinson Kratz. *Effective Listening Skills.* Chicago: Irwin Professional Publishing, 1995.

Laborde, Genie Z. *Influencing with Integrity: Management Skills for Communication and Negotiation.* Palo Alto: Syntony Publishing, 1983.

Siress, Ruth Herrman, with Carolyn Riddle and Deborah Shouse. *Working Woman's Communications Survival Guide: How to Present Your Ideas with Impact, Clarity & Power and Get the Recognition You Deserve.* Englewood Cliffs, N.J.: Prentice Hall, 1994.

7

Conducting Effective Meetings

Myrna J. McCallister

Library Director, Muhlenberg College

and

Thomas H. Patterson

Allentown, Pennsylvania

Meetings are a fact of life for most managers. It is estimated that many supervisors spend one-third to one-half of their time in meetings. Any activity that demands such a high proportion of your time deserves to be done well and thoughtfully.

The ability to chair a meeting is not instinctive. It is both a science and an art that can be taught and learned. Your meetings will reflect to a large degree your methods, manners, beliefs, and moods. Often the tone of your meetings will extend to the rest of the workplace. Studies have shown that effective chairpersons possess most or all of the following traits:

interest in, and knowledge of, the subject of the meeting and the organization,

enthusiasm for the specific topic,

leadership and the ability to motivate,

self-confidence,

follow-through,

knowledge of the subject,

power of persuasion,

sense of humor,

empathy or the ability to see others' viewpoints,

sufficient vision to distinguish major from trivial issues,

procedural know-how,

ability to focus the discussion and keep it on track.

Benefits of Good Meetings

Despite the common complaint that meetings are a waste of time, in reality little can be accomplished without a mechanism for bringing people together. Much of what is done in organizations is effected by groups who must get together to disseminate information, coordinate activities, solve problems, and make decisions. Planned and executed well, meetings can, and should, accomplish the following for a supervisor and staff:

share information,

solve problems,

eliminate time-consuming repetition in individual sessions,

generate ideas,

gain cooperation,

promote team spirit and consensus,

lessen impact of rumors,

assign responsibilities and initiate action,

provide training in new techniques and provide staff development
activities.

Over time, the act of meeting together can strengthen working relationships, encourage camaraderie, improve group and individual morale, enhance communication, motivate, and instill values in employees. Having well-orchestrated meetings with your employees can communicate to them that you value them and their input.

This chapter will provide you with guidelines for planning and conducting successful meetings. With practice and preparation you will find that your meetings will be productive for you and your staff.

Problems Resulting from Bad Meetings

Poor meetings can make a bad situation worse. There are occasions when proper discussion is curtailed or when incorrect or incomplete information leads to a bad decision. At other times, members who do not endorse a decision may say nothing out of fear or apathy. The resulting lack of cohesion can derail implementation of a group decision. It is likely that many organizational failures are due in part to flawed teamwork and flawed meetings.

One of the most serious results of poor meetings is waste. Meetings are costly, and this fact of life can get lost in service organizations such as libraries. For example, a meeting that takes workers away from the job is likely to reduce productivity. It is estimated that 40 percent to 80 percent of meeting time is wasted. Therefore, to give yourself a concrete idea of the cost of your meetings, compute how much salary per hour, per person is needed for a staff meeting. Then, if you compute a dollar amount of up to 80 percent waste, you can begin to see the loss to your department caused by bad meetings.

One bad meeting, or even a short string of them, probably won't have a lasting negative impact on your staff. Continued bad experiences, however, can have a long-term negative impact on the morale of your workers. Your career and reputation can be adversely affected as well. If meetings repeatedly result in unresolved controversy, or nothing gets accomplished, participants will take the frustration back with them to their desks. Work may give way to grumbling and complaining. In fact, the amount of time lost after meetings has been estimated to be worth $800,000 per year per 1,000 employees.[1]

Why do meetings fail? Obviously, no supervisor sets out to have a poor meeting. It is just as unlikely that meeting participants seek an unrewarding experience. Some of the leading reasons for meeting failure include the following:

- No specific objective for the meeting
- No agenda set for the meeting
- Too many, or the wrong choice of, participants
- No consideration for the roles of allies and antagonists
- Failure to prepare properly
- Inability to present ideas concisely
- Lack of sound leadership and control
- Improper use of visual aids
- Too many digressions and interruptions
- Time wasted on *why* rather than *how*
- Mixed final decisions, inconclusive discussion
- Existence of hidden agenda to divert the discussion

Alternatives to Meetings

An important first step in planning a meeting is to make sure a meeting is needed in the first place. Without a purpose, no meeting can be successful. Therefore, as a supervisor, you will want to consider carefully the need for a meeting versus alternative communication methods.

The reasons to have a meeting generally fall into five categories: (1) to inform, (2) to train, (3) to inspire, (4) to solve problems, and (5) to resolve conflict. In each of these instances you should ask yourself if there is a more effective way to meet the goal. If information dissemination is the primary objective, the distribution of a memo may do the job more economically. If staff members need to be updated on the status of various projects, you could solicit written reports from those responsible and circulate them. Problem resolution requiring only a few persons can be carried out by telephone or informal conversation.

The hardest meetings to eliminate are the regular or routine meetings held because custom or organizational culture dictate it. There is sometimes a feeling of comfort in the routine weekly or monthly staff meeting. If, as a manager, you determine that these meetings have no value to you or to your staff, you may want to consider reducing their frequency or calling them only when there is a clear need. Remember, it is obvious to all involved when the leader is filling up the agenda with topics of little interest or importance.

Generally, you should not have a meeting when

the subject matter is so confidential or tentative that it cannot be shared;

there are incomplete data available, or you are poorly prepared for potential questions;

something could be communicated better by telephone, memo, report, or a one-on-one discussion;

the subject is too trivial; or

there is currently too much anger or hostility in the group and people need time to calm down before they can work together effectively.

What to Do before the Meeting

The most crucial part of any meeting takes place before the meeting begins. Advance preparation should be the most time-consuming activity of the meeting. First formulate the objective(s) of the meeting. You should be able to state the objective clearly, indicate what the meeting should accomplish, and explain your reason for calling the meeting. It is a good idea to write this down to clarify your thinking. Gather all pertinent facts about the issue at hand. Use all the information resources available, from literature to colleagues to experts. You must appear to be, and be, confident. This is only possible if you are fully briefed. In gathering information, try to imagine any questions you might be asked. If you can't get the information needed to provide an answer, be prepared to say why.

Make sure you and the participants know the meeting rules beforehand. For example, if you have a rule against accepting telephone calls during the meeting, everyone should be made aware of it. Furthermore, be sure you know and understand the rules and procedures of the organization. Identify your allies and discuss tactics and strategies with them. Consider all potential areas of conflict and think about how to deal with them.

Ensure that attendees are prepared by distributing advance reports or other handouts before the meeting, perhaps accompanying the agenda. Make it clear what should be done with the background material before the meeting; that is, read it, think about it, make comments on it, bring it with you, circulate it for comment. Unless it is an emergency, don't hand out lengthy information during the meeting.

Prepare the Agenda

The blueprint for your meeting is the written agenda. Only in emergency situations should you try to have a meeting without one. If you feel your meeting is too unimportant to warrant an agenda, your participants will feel it is trivial as well. The agenda constitutes a contract among all the participants concerning their mutual purpose and methods.

What are the characteristics of effective agendas? Although the form, length, and detail may vary according to the circumstances, you should consider the following points:

TIMING

The agenda should go out with sufficient lead time to allow participants to prepare. Don't, however, send it out so far in advance that people forget about it. In most cases, three to five working days ahead of the meeting should suffice.

DISTRIBUTION

The agenda should go to all participants. Some supervisors think they have more control if they alone have an agenda, but this is an ineffective means of control. You may also have colleagues or supervisors who would like to see an advance copy.

ITEMS

Avoid broad topics as agenda items. State items so that the focus of the discussion is clear.

ALLOCATION OF DISCUSSION TIME

In addition to start and stop times for the meeting, you may want to indicate specific time allocations for each item.

RESPONSIBILITY FOR AGENDA ITEMS

If you want certain people to present specific information such as statistics, make sure this is noted on the agenda. You might consider making various attendees responsible for chairing a portion of the agenda to add variety and increase group participation.

ORDER OF ITEMS

Determining the sequence of items to be discussed gives a great deal of power to the chair. Do you want to get an unpleasant topic over with soon? Place it at the beginning of the agenda. Do you hope to avoid lengthy discussion of a sensitive item? Place it near the end of the agenda. Experiment with the order of agenda items to find what works best.

Some supervisors have developed their own agenda form to help them prepare for a meeting. Such a form assembles on one page all pertinent information concerning the meeting. Try developing your own form, including the following:

- Name of group
- Title of meeting (such as "biweekly department meeting")
- Person calling the meeting
- Date, starting time, place
- Ending time
- Meeting type (problem solving, decision making, planning, reporting, reaction)
- Desired outcome(s)
- Background materials
- Items to bring
- Group members (and guests, if applicable)
- Decision-making method and final decision maker
- Order of agenda items, persons responsible, and time allocated to each

Decide on the Participants

An important rule of thumb in deciding who should come to a meeting is "the fewer the participants, the more effective the meeting." This rule pertains largely to problem-solving or training meetings, where a large group is harder to focus, and communication can be confusing or time-consuming. It is to your advantage to keep the meeting limited to as few participants as needed to get the job done. In deciding whom to invite, consider who understands the issue; who has the power to make a decision; who will be responsible for implementing a decision; and who will be affected by decisions taken.

Sometimes "other people" are invited just because of a leader's vague feeling that they "ought to be involved." Resist this. Frequently the effectiveness of a meeting is reduced because unnecessary people are present and the necessary ones weren't invited or can't make it. If even one person who is essential can't make it, reschedule the meeting. You will find that progress can't be made without all the essential people, and you will have to repeat your effort later. You may want to consider the following questions in deciding whom to invite.

- Whom are you obligated to invite?
- Who can give you what you want?
- Who is in favor of your objective?
- Who will oppose your objective?
- Who is on the fence?
- Who can cause trouble if not invited?

Sometimes the regular staff meeting can become routine, and the leader may add variety by inviting an occasional guest. A homogeneous group that has met together for some time can fall into "groupthink" patterns that are as insidious as they are difficult to identify. Bringing in new participants such as experts, people from other divisions, visiting librarians, or vendors can help prevent or restrain groupthink. Not only does new blood inject more life into groups and put everyone on good behavior, it also helps to break down communication barriers and prevent the formation of subgroups.

Factors to Consider

Adequate managers know how to deal with the concrete and factual details of meetings, such as information gathering and timely agenda distribution. Truly effective managers have learned the importance of weighing, balancing, and taking advantage of more subtle factors, such as the following:

ROOM ARRANGEMENT

When chairs are uncomfortable or not thoughtfully arranged, minds will wander. The ideal chair is not too comfortable or too uncomfortable. If the meeting is small, people should be seated so that they can face each other. Circle arrangements symbolize equality and the importance of each person. When a person is seated at the "head" of an arrangement, this person is perceived to be in a superior position. A U-shaped formation is often preferred for larger groups of twelve to twenty-five. Adversaries should be seated side by side where they don't have eye contact, reducing the potential for conflict. If you want to gain support from someone, try to sit directly opposite this person so that you make frequent eye contact.

PHYSICAL FACTORS

Bright light versus soft light; cool temperature versus stuffy environment; availability and quality of food and drink; comfortable easy chair versus straight chair: by combining and controlling these factors, you can influence the mood of participants. You may want to encourage a feeling of well-being if dealing with a difficult issue. If time is critical, you may not want your participants to feel so comfortable. An ideal room will be well ventilated, perhaps a bit cool, well lighted, and contain minimal distractions.

ORGANIZATIONAL FACTORS

If the organization values participatory management and consensus, then your meetings may be more frequent and longer. If the organization values results and the bottom line, then you may be considered weak if you coddle your employees in weekly meetings with coffee and doughnuts. If the organization values communication, then your minutes may be more detailed and more widely distributed. If your organization blames people for making mistakes and acting slowly, then you might get less input from your employees and have less time to gain employee consensus.

MEETING TIME

If you want to prevent the meeting from dragging, call it for 11 A.M. or 4 P.M., when the normal lunch hour or quitting time will encourage participants to wind down. To get people to show up on time, some managers schedule a meeting at an odd time, such as 2:10 P.M., because it is more memorable. Most people are at their freshest in the morning. Having a meeting first thing Monday morning or last thing Friday afternoon is not usually a good idea.

It's hard to determine an ideal length of time for a meeting, but most productive meetings run from 60 to 120 minutes. If you go over an hour and a half, schedule a bathroom-and-stretch break.

PSYCHOLOGICAL FACTORS

Factors that can have an impact on the pace or tone of the meeting and the mood of the participants include the time of year (is it the busy season?), other demands on participants' time, the presence of hostile participants, and the frequency of interruptions such as telephone calls.

What to Do during the Meeting

If proper advance planning has taken place, all that remains to be done is to steer and conduct the actual meeting, keeping events on course.

SET THE TONE

A general spirit of competency can be set or marred in the first few minutes. A short time devoted to making the participants welcome and putting them at ease will help encourage better thinking.

ENFORCE THE AGENDA

Start on time, don't wait for latecomers, and don't recap the meeting for latecomers. This wastes the time of those who arranged to arrive on time and encourages late arrivals. Make sure you adjourn on time. Bring extra copies of the agenda (and other handouts) because some are likely to forget their own. Generally, stick to the time allotted for each agenda item.

KEEP MINUTES

You may not want to record the meeting yourself, but make sure someone is responsible for keeping track of the events of the meeting.

KEEP THE MEETING FOCUSED

Summarize the discussion and the conclusions reached after each agenda item. Be miserly with meeting time. Don't allow private meetings within meetings. Ask questions. Draw out quiet members and control talkative ones. Don't give your opinion too soon or you might discourage input.

INTERRUPT IF NECESSARY

You may need to interrupt to get the floor and regain control of the meeting. To interrupt, raise your hand and say, "Just a second, may I . . ." and continue speaking. You may also interrupt by standing. The person speaking will usually pause, and you can say, "John, another point . . ." and continue talking. Another method is to begin to speak, raising your voice consistently higher. Make sure you listen more than you talk. No one should talk for longer than fifteen minutes at a stretch, even when training or giving a presentation.

AVOID GROUPTHINK

Watch for symptoms of groupthink, such as reticence to challenge the majority opinion or interpreting silence as approval. You can challenge the majority opinion by playing devil's advocate or by assigning someone to play this role.

BE ALERT TO GROUP DYSFUNCTION

Watch for signs of problems in the group dynamics. These may include avoidance of the task, impatience, attacking ideas before they are fully expressed, disagreement and polarization, subtle interpersonal attacks, a rise or drop in noise level, difficulty in making a decision, the entrance of a new member or exit of an old member, and poor eye contact.

MAKE THE MEETING INTERESTING

Remember that visuals will increase retention and add variety to the meeting. Your use of audiovisual materials need not be elaborate. A blackboard or flip chart can be effective.

CONTROL YOURSELF

As chair, you set the tone. You may become embarrassed, angry, exasperated, or overstressed. But it is generally a very bad idea to show it. Insist that other participants follow your lead in controlling themselves.

WRAP-UP

Close the meeting on time and on a positive note. Summarize the major activity of the meeting and recap responsibility for further action.

What to Do after the Meeting

A perfectly planned and well-executed meeting is still a failure if no result comes of it. It is the chair's responsibility to ensure that all participants understand the outcome of the meeting, that follow-up is assigned and monitored, and that the meeting is evaluated for potential improvements.

MINUTES

Minutes are the best way to ensure a common understanding of the meeting and of follow-up responsibilities. Minutes should go out promptly so everyone knows what was accomplished. You may choose to use a "meeting action sheet" to replace formal minutes. This form would include name of group, objectives, agenda items, who attended, decisions reached, action required, person responsible for action, and completion date for action. A form highlights succinctly the decisions reached and is easy for participants to read and retain. Even if you need formal minutes, a form can be used as a cover sheet to summarize the meeting.

EVALUATE THE MEETING

You may do this evaluation informally, simply by thinking about the meeting. Often it helps to write down your evaluation, listing alternative ways you could have handled a particular issue.

FOLLOW-UP

Periodically, get out the minutes or "meeting action sheet" and track progress on the items. If progress is not being made, find out why and get the action back on track.

By following the guidelines in this chapter, you can plan and lead effective meetings.

Suggestions for handling particular problems that may arise during a meeting are given in the next section. At the end of the chapter is a Checklist for Meeting Planners summarizing actions to be taken before, during, and after a meeting.

Handling Problems

How should you handle specific problems during a meeting you chair?

What if a staff member always reacts with negative comments to any suggestion during your meetings?

As chair of the meeting you usually have the freedom to rephrase those comments in a positive way and try to make them more action oriented. You could say, "Sue, you've done a thorough job of pointing out a potential problem we need to watch for. What constructive advice could you give for avoiding this?" This tactic can put the negative person in a position of saying something positive.

What if a staff member never says anything at meetings?

The chair can make a point of asking staff members to submit in writing a few ideas on agenda topics before the meeting. This has the advantage of focusing staff members on the issues and may make it easier for them to speak up in the meeting. If, however, a staff member still remains silent, the chair can say, "Well, Paul, you had a good idea on this topic. Let's discuss it with everyone."

Another method for getting people to participate is to ask direct questions. Make sure the questions are specific rather than general and not answerable by a yes or no. Direct your questions to an individual, using that individual's name rather than tossing out a question vaguely to the group.

What can you do about a person who talks too much?

You may not want to silence this person totally, but only get him or her to reduce the quantity of comments. You may later want to take advantage of a person willing and able to talk when the conversation lags and you need someone to break the ice. But if you are troubled with an over-talker, silence the person firmly.

How can you get an attendee who has wandered off to a different topic back on track?

Point to the agenda and ask pleasantly but straightforwardly how the point relates to the issues being discussed. Generally, the person will see that he or she has moved away from the item, apologize, and give up the floor. But if the person persists, you may want to say, "That's a good point, but we don't have time to discuss it at this meeting. Will you please see me about it after the meeting?"

One person could be assigned the duty of seeing that all group members stay on the subject. Having it understood that a specific person is responsible for keeping to the agenda may make such reminders seem less rude. This person could say, "We only have a short time left. I'll make a note of this topic and set up a meeting to discuss it later. But for now, let's get back to . . . ." This also allows the chair to concentrate on the meeting and to seem less like a police officer.

Some chairs will save five to fifteen minutes at the end of the meeting to allow for discussion of extraneous topics that emerge during the meeting. Some or all of these may be placed on the agenda for the next meeting.

What if a participant at a meeting really doesn't like you and is trying to needle you or make you look bad?

Treat the troublemaker with some of his or her own medicine. At first you may want to join in the fun, trading quip for quip, but keep calm and keep smiling. If the behavior continues and is disrupting the meeting, you may have to silence the troublemaker. By this point, most of the attendees will be on your side and will approve of your silencing the needler. If this is an ongoing pattern, you may wish to enlist the help of an ally in silencing the person.

Note

1. Michael Doyle and David Straus, *How to Make Meetings Work* (New York: Jove, 1982), 9.

Suggested Reading

Contributed by Lucinda Daily, University of Alabama Libraries.

Anderson, Karen. *The Busy Manager's Guide to Successful Meetings.* Hawthorne, N.J.: Career Press, 1993.

Burleson, Clyde W. *Effective Meetings: The Complete Guide.* New York: Wiley, 1990.

Chang, Richard Y., and Kevin R. Kehoe. *Meetings That Work: A Practical Guide to Shorter More Productive Meetings.* Irvine, Calif.: Richard Chang Associates, 1993.

Daniels, William R. *Orchestrating Powerful Regular Meetings: A Manager's Complete Guide.* San Diego, Calif.: Pfeiffer and Company, 1993.

Hackett, Donald, and Charles L. Martin. *Facilitation Skills for Team Leaders.* Menlo Park, Calif.: Crisp Publications, 1993.

Lippincott, Sharon M. *Meetings Dos, Don'ts and Donuts: The Complete Handbook for Successful Meetings.* Pittsburgh, Penn.: Lighthouse Point Press, 1994.

Rae, Leslie. *Let's Have a Meeting: A Comprehensive Guide to Making Your Meetings Work.* New York: McGraw-Hill, 1994.

Shelton, Marie M., and Laurie K. Bauer. *Secrets of Highly Effective Meetings.* Thousand Oaks, Calif.: Corwin Press, 1994.

Checklist for Meeting Planners

Before the Meeting

Formulate objectives.

Write down specific goal statements, making them quantitative where possible.

Determine if a meeting is necessary to meet objectives.

Compose a list of attendees, inviting the minimum necessary.

Decide the date and time for the meeting, and verify it with attendees.

Decide the meeting place and arrangement of the room; inspect it personally.

Check budget details, if applicable.

Arrange for physical environment (A/V, food, lighting, etc.).

Examine program content: What ideas need to be communicated? What needs to be accomplished? Who is the best person to present program content?

Determine methods of presentation and arrange for A/V needs.

Communicate with presenters and attendees.

Arrange for a recorder or minute-taker.

Distribute the agenda and other advance documents.

During the Meeting

Make appropriate introductions.

Start on time; don't recap for latecomers.

Set the tone for the meeting; review purpose and meeting rules.

Agree on the agenda and time frame; announce any changes to, or reorganization of, the items on the agenda.

Schedule appropriate breaks if meeting exceeds ninety minutes.

Hold back on expressing your opinions too early in the meeting.

Draw out quiet members; don't allow others to dominate.

See that each item on the agenda has some resolution.

Have minutes taken to record actions, decisions, and planned follow-up.

$\longrightarrow$

Agree on follow-up action; assure that such action is assigned and recorded.

Summarize major accomplishments of the meeting.

End the meeting on time.

After the Meeting

Critique the meeting, alone or with participant input.

Distribute minutes or "meeting action summary"; report on or publicize the meeting.

Implement decisions.

Follow up on implementation.

Evaluate results.

8

Managing Work Time

Mary Nofsinger

Head of Reference
Washington State University Library

After the initial thrill of promotion has worn off, a new supervisor frequently feels overwhelmed with the quantity and complexity of responsibilities, activities, and decisions which must now be handled. You soon realize there's never enough time to get everything done. You get further and further behind and time becomes a valuable commodity. Time cannot be stored, bought, or rented. Although your daily allotment of time cannot be increased, it can be managed to provide more job satisfaction and a sense of control and achievement. This chapter offers suggestions for managing time related to various supervisory tasks including long-range planning, decision making, and delegating, as well as effectively utilizing your personal work time.

Planning: Setting Goals and Establishing Priorities

Planning plays a vital role in supervisory success. It is a way of connecting the future with the present and provides a means of controlling what work we do and the order in which we do it.[1] It involves setting specific unit goals and objectives, establishing priorities, and then following through so that unit goals and objectives become integrated with the organizational mission.

Setting Goals and Objectives

Overall library goals are usually developed by higher-level administrators, as part of strategic plans. These plans establish systemwide priorities, set future direction, and provide a framework for tactical plans. Most supervisors are involved primarily with tactical plans, also called action plans.[2] Action plans assist the organization in achieving goals related to strategic plans, such as the implementation of programs and projects at lower levels in the library system. As a supervisor, you will need to develop unit goals and objectives which address action plans, as well as your own personal goals. Below are ten basic guidelines for developing goals:[3]

1. Identify what needs to be done. Be specific and absolutely clear about what you want to achieve. Encourage employees to work with you to help set goals that can be measured objectively.
2. Review unit goals to ensure they are in harmony with the overall mission of the library. Check library goals against your employees' values. If goals are not in harmony with employees' personal values, progress may be sabotaged.
3. Analyze unit goals in regard to the availability of needed resources—people, time, and money. Calculate risks and tradeoffs. Then, develop realistic strategies to achieve desirable goals.
4. Estimate how much time is needed to complete each goal by working backward from the target date. List tasks needed to be accomplished in reverse order.
5. Set timetables for accomplishing goals, either short- or long-term. Involve staff in this process on a regular basis. They are often more realistic about timetables since they have more firsthand experience with the tasks to be accomplished.

6. Chart or write down unit goals so you can visualize them better. Encourage employees to do the same.

7. Set priorities among goals (see section below). List only the most important goals that will make a significant difference in what you want to achieve. To be successful, both the supervisor and employees must have the same general understanding of priorities for unit work.

8. Build in a reward system for achieving goals. Make an effort to give your staff some individual, personal recognition when goals are accomplished. Also reward teamwork.

9. Take action daily to move closer toward goals.

10. Regularly review the list of unit goals. Revise them as values and priorities change. Also review staff goals as part of the regular employee evaluation process.

Establishing Priorities

Time management involves prioritizing the tasks that are most important to you and your unit. The supervisor usually makes the final decision on which tasks are high, medium, and low priority. If a task directly supports the achievement of an important goal, assign it a high priority. Make a list of the high-priority tasks, and use this list to provide direction for daily work. Here are some tips for getting started:[4]

1. Get into a planning routine. Take five or ten minutes each day, either just before you leave work in the evening or first thing in the morning of the current day, to plan for accomplishing high-priority tasks. Encourage your staff also to take time for daily planning.

2. Set priorities a day ahead, if at all possible. Encourage your employees to do the same. Sometimes our minds assist in resolving issues as we sleep.

3. Schedule time to deal with top-priority issues daily. Don't just react to whatever the day brings. Allow extra time in your schedule to address unexpected, high-priority issues your employees bring to you.

4. Be flexible. As circumstances change from day to day, so must priorities. Anticipating possible changes in advance is contingency planning.

5. Consider staff workloads when assigning or delegating priority tasks. Be realistic about how much time will be needed, to avoid unnecessary employee stress.

6. Revise personnel priorities regularly. As a supervisor, you need to assist employees daily with revising their priorities. The more supervisors and staff can support the completion of each others' priority tasks, the closer they will come to attaining unit goals.

7. Consider long-term career objectives when setting daily priorities. Remember that issues which are urgent (those demanding your immediate attention) are often not important for promotion or professional development.

8. Keep a written list of each day's priorities in a prominent place as a constant reminder to yourself to focus your efforts on what is most important.

Finally, there is no perfect way to track progress or accomplishments. Some experts suggest that you work on your first priority issue until it is finished. Others suggest that you tackle the hardest job first. Still others suggest that you split up your available time among equally important tasks. Whatever system you use, ask yourself the classic time management question throughout each day, "What is the best use of my time right now?"

Decision Making

A supervisor spends large quantities of time making daily decisions regarding both minor and major issues. Timely decision making is facilitated by doing relevant research and evaluating the risks associated with different options. Here are four preliminary steps to help you navigate the decision-making process.[5]

1. Diagnose the problem. Identify and clarify the nature of the issue and its causes. Get background information from your employees and determine what other relevant data need to be

obtained. State your requirements for a satisfactory solution, including time limitations.

2. Determine who should make the decision. If the issue has systemwide implications, you may want to consult with a superior. At other times, decisions should be made by group consensus or majority vote, which may take longer but often ensures greater cooperation and less risk of sabotage. If the decision falls within your specific areas of responsibility, then take the initiative and proceed.

3. Consider possible solutions. One alternative is to deliberately choose inaction, to back off and see what happens. Other creative alternatives include finding a way around the difficulty, removing the problem, or changing your attitude toward the situation. If appropriate to the problem, ask your employees to brainstorm ideas for prospective solutions at a staff meeting. Consider as many options as possible within your time limitations.

4. Analyze the best options under the specific circumstances. Carefully compare the advantages and disadvantages of the most promising options prior to taking action. Consult with your employees when appropriate. Ask yourself the following questions in order to make the best decision:

- If you proceed with a particular decision, what is likely to happen?
- Is the anticipated result worth implementing?
- What are the probable risks?
- If there are no good alternatives, should you do nothing?

To fulfill job expectations as a supervisor, you need to make rational, timely decisions. Thus, you will frequently have to cope with fear of failure, the desire to make an extended analysis of the situation (there's never enough time to consider all factors), a preference for "waiting for the best time" (it seldom occurs), and inherent tendencies toward procrastination. Ultimately, being a supervisor includes accepting the responsibility for making prompt decisions, developing an implementation strategy, and being accountable for the specific results achieved.

Delegating

Delegation is entrusting an employee or team member to act on your behalf. The employee acts as your agent and has responsibility for performing defined tasks or activities. For librarians who supervise other employees, delegation is an essential element of time management. Delegation frequently begins with a supervisor asking, "Which of my activities could be handled by someone else just as well, if not better?"

If used effectively, delegation can increase employee job satisfaction, provide variety and novelty, develop employee skills and promotion potential, improve productivity, and result in effective decisions at the most appropriate level.[6] Here are eight factors a supervisor should consider prior to delegating:

1. Identify appropriate work to be delegated. Do nothing yourself that could just as well be delegated to an employee.

2. Do not delegate unnecessary tasks. Ask yourself, "Does this task really need to be done by anyone?"

3. Both authority and responsibility must be delegated if a task is to be carried out effectively.

4. Plan ahead and parcel out the work in advance of deadlines so you have time to review or revise.

5. Focus on results and do not "micromanage." Your employee needs freedom of action to perform the job well.

6. Always acknowledge and give full credit to the person who does the work. The employee's success reflects well on you, too.

7. Ultimately, responsibility for results remains with the person who delegates. The buck stops on your desk if there are problems.

8. Know what *not* to delegate:

   - Activities that are most important (highest priority or risk) to you.
   - Sensitive issues that may have serious personnel or legal implications, such as disciplinary action, confidential matters, etc.

- Activities concerned with change and/or instability in the organization. Stable issues are easier for others to handle.
- Thinking, planning, and innovating aspects of a supervisory job. In contrast, routine issues and periodic problems can usually be delegated.

After considering the factors above, a new supervisor will quickly realize that delegating skills need to be learned. Part of a supervisor's job is to train employees for promotion and to get the best results possible. Here are ten steps for effective delegation:[7]

1. Define the goal or task succinctly, preferably in writing.
2. Select the right person for the job to be delegated. This person must have the right attitude and aptitude. Experience should not be the sole criterion.
3. Discuss the scope of the job from beginning to end with the employee, including the specific results you expect.
4. Agree on a process and make arrangements for proper training.
5. Agree on authority and responsibility. Good delegating includes transferring control and responsibility to the person who performs the work.
6. Agree on limitations, parameters, and resources to be provided.
7. Establish a reporting procedure so you will be kept informed of progress at regular intervals. Also monitor progress informally by asking "How's it going?" whenever an appropriate opportunity arises.
8. Set control checkpoints. Perhaps you will want to delegate tasks in progressive phases to allow for review and revision at crucial points in the process.
9. Agree on specific time schedules and deadlines.
10. Follow through. Discuss problems, give feedback, coach and counsel the employee. Sometimes an employee's initial performance may be unsatisfactory. If so, you will need to intervene and take corrective action as you counsel the employee. Monitor the situation without appearing to oversupervise. Delegate additional parts of the job to the employee, if necessary.

In conjunction with delegating, supervisors frequently use a technique called *management by wandering around* to keep themselves continually informed of employee progress.[8] It usually saves supervisory time to make sure that a job gets done right initially, rather than spending time to make corrections later. Remember, high-level employee performance always reflects well on the supervisor.

Managing Personal Time

After dealing with organizational demands from superiors, coworkers, and employees, supervisors probably have less than 25 percent of their working hours free for "discretionary" or personal use.[9] There are a variety of personal time-management techniques that can help you accomplish more of your high priority tasks each day. Don't try to do everything at once. Pick and choose the techniques that fit best with your own personality and the work environment at your particular institution.

Record and Analyze Activities

To manage time, you need to get an accurate sense of how you are actually using time in different daily activities. There are numerous examples of time log forms available.[10] Record how you spend your time for at least two weeks, preferably several times a year. To analyze the results, set up categories of frequent activity, such as meetings, handling mail, and so forth. Tally the amount of time you spend on each type of activity. Then, ask yourself three questions:[11]

- What am I doing that really does not need to be done at all—by me or anyone else?
- Which of the activities on my time log could be handled by someone else just as well, if not better?
- What do I do that wastes the time of others?

Use the results of your analysis to pinpoint where time is wasted and to identify work to be delegated. Then, examine your daily schedule to focus your use of time and increase productivity.

Develop a Daily "To-Do" List

Starting with the goals and objectives that have already been established, an efficient supervisor develops an action plan each day. Use a notebook, a planner (usually a ring binder with separate sections for calendars, phone numbers, etc.), a time-management diary, or a PDA (personal digital assistant) if you prefer electronic access and keep it with you at all times.

1. Make preparing your daily list a habit. Do it at the same time each day.

2. Add items from your "follow-up" system or tickler file—reminders about tasks to be done on certain days, such as letters, notes, phone messages, preparing meeting papers, etc.

3. Determine your peak performance hours during the day and schedule the most creative and vital activities during prime periods.

4. Focus on objectives and schedule highest priority tasks first. Block in appointments with yourself to work on these tasks.

5. Batch similar tasks, especially those that have little impact on your key goals, and do them all at once. As you reach momentum, you can finish them quickly.

6. Try to schedule "quiet time" for yourself every day—time to think and plan.

7. Use transition time productively—utilize spare time while you wait for appointments, commute to work, etc.

8. Allow yourself some flexibility to deal with the unexpected.

9. Use today's "To-Do" list as the starting point for tomorrow's list.

10. Try to do a little "elephant eating" each day; that is, tackle a small portion of your highest priority goal. It's usually impossible to deal with a large task entirely at one sitting, so "start chewing" on a smaller part of it.[12]

Manage Paperwork Effectively

Paper shuffling can be a serious time-management problem for supervisors because it frequently detracts from more important tasks to be done. Clear objectives will be your guide to what to retain and what to throw away. As you work, constantly ask your-self, "How do I plan to use this piece of paper or file?" Here are three time-tested rules for an efficient system:

RULE ONE

Handle each piece of paper or file only once. When you pick up an item, do not put it back in your in-box without taking some action to move it toward its final disposition. If you are prone to procrastination, use the measles method; every time you handle a piece of paper, put a dot in the upper left corner. This provides a visual cue to move things along, especially after three or four dots appear.[13]

RULE TWO

Examine each piece of paper or file received and decide which should be kept, referred or delegated to someone else, or tossed in the trash. Those items needing your action should be sorted into three piles for efficient handling, such as A (Urgent), B (Soon), and C (Reading).[14] The A items should be given your highest priority for action. Keep putting them on your daily "To-Do" list until they are totally completed.

The B items may be put in a "hold" or "pending" file near your desk for action within the next several days—most corre-spondence will fall into this category. When handling correspon-dence, it is often efficient to write your response on the letter or memo received and photocopy it for your records. While you may draft correspondence on your word processor, delegate the typing and formatting of the final copy to a secretary or other support staff. Consider using form letters, constructed with standard para-graphs which you have used in previous letters, for routine inquiries, confirmations, and rejection letters. Also try to develop standardized forms containing checklists or boxes to tick for reports or any document that much be created on a regular basis.

The C items, the reading pile, should be scrutinized closely according to two criteria: Will it contribute to attaining your pro-fessional goals? If not, then it is probably not worth using work time to read it. Does it contain something useful? Scan the pref-ace, the introduction, the table of contents, the index, summaries, conclusion, and perhaps the first line of several paragraphs. When you select an item, allocate a time and a place for your reading, perhaps fifteen minutes to an hour during a less busy time of day after priority A tasks have been completed. Always keep reading materials in your briefcase and read while traveling or waiting for an appointment or meeting.

RULE THREE

When finished with action items, evaluate which papers or files should be retained. With either paper or electronic storage systems, easy access to the information is the main reason for filing. Alphabetic (subject) filing systems are most popular for topics such as annual review, promotion, and disciplinary actions. Chronological filing systems are useful for daily, monthly, or annually recurring events. To maintain your system and keep it up to date, follow some simple procedures:

1. Make sure there is a date on each item and a brief note regarding any actions you have already taken.
2. File promptly. Ideally, each item should be filed as soon as a decision is made, while your rationale is clear. If this is not possible, then set up a to-be-filed box and take care of this task once a week.
3. Decide what to file. Be conscious of legal or organizational requirements for retention, particularly with documents related to supervisory responsibilities.
4. When in doubt, throw it out. Keep only items that are original and cannot easily be duplicated, items that others are not required to keep, and items that you expect to need in the future.
5. Identify how long something will be needed and anticipate whether it should be stored in active, inactive, or dead files.
6. Keep the most recent papers or files in front in your filing system.
7. Compile a list of subjects or an index and put it in the front of your file.
8. After using a file, put each item back as soon as you are finished with it. If files are shared, develop a reliable charge-out system.

9. Each time you add new items to a file, spend a minute sifting through the file and disposing of superseded material.

Keep a Neat Desk

A cluttered desk holds many potential distractions. In order to keep more focused, your desk should be clear of other papers except for the project at hand. Here are some suggestions for eliminating clutter:

1. Monitor your in-box frequently and keep items from accumulating. Promptly sort items received into the three categories mentioned earlier (A, B, C).

2. Always know what is on your desk. Unidentified pieces of paper create delays when you want to find something in a hurry.

3. Clean off your desk regularly. If desperate, sort excess material into three boxes: Priority, Routine, and Reading. When your desk is clean, immediately start working on the items in the Priority box.

Use Large Blocks of Time

Personal time should be concentrated into good-sized chunks in order to allow uninterrupted work on highest priority tasks. There are many ways of consolidating time. Some supervisors work at home one day a week. Others schedule several mornings a week to work on major projects. Others take work home in the evening (not recommended due to fatigue). It takes a lot of self-discipline to push secondary matters aside, estimate how many hours are needed to wrestle with a project, and then take the necessary time to finish the project. Effective supervisors learn to concentrate their work efforts on activities that will have the greatest impact.

Minimize Unnecessary Interruptions

While some interruptions are unavoidable for keeping your unit functioning smoothly, a supervisor must often balance the need to be available to staff and other drop-in visitors against the need for more time to concentrate on high-priority tasks. Here are some helpful guidelines:

1. Deal with unit problems and issues *before* they become major crises requiring additional time and effort to resolve.

2. Schedule regular meetings with your staff to discuss unit business, to check priorities, and to establish procedures and policies in a timely manner.

3. Set fixed times each day when you have an "open-door" policy and encourage employees to bring work-related matters to you during these hours.

4. Set fixed times each day when a "closed-door" policy is in effect. Post these hours to avoid being interrupted by staff and other visitors.

5. If you cannot avoid interruption, write a quick note to yourself so you do not lose your train of thought when you want to get back on track later. Try to carry a notepad with you at all times to record unexpected requests as people stop you.

6. Have some interruption-beating phrases you have rehearsed in advance, such as:

   "I'm busy now, but I'll get back to you . . ."

   "Let's make this quick since I need to finish . . ."

7. As for telephone interruptions, ask your secretary or an employee to screen calls and take messages during your "closed-door" time.

8. If you have voice mail, just do not answer the phone during the hours you are unavailable. Use this as a last resort since it is usually more time-efficient to deal with issues immediately rather than to delay.

9. Set up a file folder for each employee who reports to you. In this folder, accumulate items for discussion at a meeting later. Then, keep the meeting brief and focused.

Learn to Say "No"

Supervisors need to learn that trying to please everyone often results in pleasing no one. The single most effective timesaving word in the English language is "no." Time is your most precious resource, so do not hesitate to say "no" to low-payoff tasks and activities that are not compatible with your own personal goals and priorities or those of the library. If this is difficult, practice, practice, practice in front of a mirror. Always be polite, but firm. It often helps to explain briefly why you are declining a request or to suggest other alternatives or options.

Avoid Procrastination

Procrastination is delaying, deferring, or putting off tasks that need to be done. It frequently causes significant personal stress, as well as poor employee performance ratings from superiors. Here's a brief checklist of reasons why procrastination may occur.[15]

- Feeling overwhelmed by the size of a task.
- Fearing failure and being judged on your performance.
- Fearing success because the reward will be more hard work.
- Seeking perfection and not knowing how to achieve it.
- Fearing loss of autonomy or control.
- The project has a high payoff but also high risk.
- The task is boring.
- The task is unpleasant.
- The task is important but not urgent.
- Low self-esteem.
- Failing to understand or accept responsibility.
- Lack of self-discipline and control.
- Feeling overburdened with a large workload.
- Lack of information.

If procrastination becomes a persistent habit in your unit, use a notebook to record the circumstances under which it occurs—the who, what, where, when, why, and how. Here are some techniques that may help break the inertia of procrastination:

1. Set strict personal rules against taking work home at night and weekends and working late. This will force you and your employees to focus on priority tasks during the day.

2. Make a realistic appraisal of the situation. Do you and your employees have the knowledge and skills needed? Can you

delegate more? Can certain tasks be eliminated? Focus on only one high priority task at a time.

3. Break a task into individual components and concrete steps. Then plan a schedule, step by step, for the project. Start on one small identifiable portion.

4. Consider the "worst-first" rather than the "worst-last" approach. Identify the worst parts of a task and focus on them first. Then the remainder of the task will be easier to accomplish.

5. Set small deadlines and reward yourself and your employees after each accomplishment.

6. Use visible reminders—stick-on notes, red flags, etc. These will continually remind you and your employees to focus on a task.

7. Consider sharing the burden by involving others in your activity.

8. Make a public commitment to complete a task by a certain date. Going public often keeps you more focused, especially if you dread failure.

9. Give yourself a penalty by agreeing to give up something you like if you do not start your task by a certain time. Discipline yourself to work until you eventually get it done.

Unfortunately, time that has already passed can never be regained, and future time is beyond our prediction. The present time is what counts. Now is when we must accomplish results in the workplace. Supervisors have to face this time reality personally and then help employees focus on the present.

Conclusion

Time management is obviously not a panacea for many of the problems plaguing libraries today. However, "one road to increased productivity is through efficient time management."[16] In addition to better productivity, learning time-management skills can help supervisors deal more effectively with stress and assist with balancing professional and personal priorities. By utilizing time-management techniques, supervisors and employees can share work knowledge and experiences more effectively, complete high-priority tasks, and experience increased self-esteem and increased career satisfaction. Remember always to ask yourself, "What is the best use of my time right now?"

Notes

1. Lynne Wenig, *The A to Z of Time Management* (Sydney, Australia: Allen & Unwin, 1993), 103.

2. Dian Walster, *Managing Time: A How-to-Do-It Manual for Librarians* (New York: Neal-Schuman, 1993), 125.

3. Wenig, op. cit., 64–65.

4. J. Wesley Cochran, *Time Management Handbook for Librarians* (New York: Greenwood Press, 1992), 21–24.

5. Ross A. Webber, *Time and Management* (New York: Moffat Publishing, 1981), 95.

6. Wenig, op. cit., 36–37.

7. Ibid., 38.

8. Cochran, op. cit., 84.

9. Peter F. Drucker, "How to Manage Your Time," *Harper's Magazine* 233 (December 1966): 56.

10. Two books containing time log forms are: Sheila Creth and the Association of Research Libraries, *Conducting Effective Meetings and Other Time Management Techniques* (Chicago: American Library Association, 1982) and J. Wesley Cochran, *Time Management Handbook for Librarians*.

11. Drucker, op. cit., 57.

12. Wenig, op. cit., 49.

13. Cochran, op. cit., 37.

14. Walster, op. cit., 94.

15. Wenig, op. cit., 111–13.

16. Helen M. Gothberg and Donald E. Riggs, "Time Management in Academic Libraries," *College and Research Libraries* 49 (March 1988): 131.

Suggested Reading

Cochran, J. Wesley. *Time Management Handbook for Librarians*. New York: Greenwood Press, 1992.

Douglass, Merrill E., and Donna N. Douglass. *Manage Your Time, Your Work, Yourself*. New York: AMACOM, 1993.

Walster, Dian. *Managing Time: A How-to-Do-It Manual for Librarians*. New York: Neal-Schuman, 1993.

Wenig, Lynne. *The A to Z of Time Management*. Sydney, Australia: Allen & Unwin, 1993, p. 103.

Williams, Paul B. *Getting a Project Done on Time: Managing People, Time, and Results*. New York: AMACOM, 1996.

9

Managing Diversity

Marilyn Okrent

Director of Human Resources
Queens Borough Public Library

A primary goal of diversity in libraries is to develop a productive workforce that can best serve a diverse customer base. The increasing use of technology makes it more important than ever to strengthening the position of libraries as information providers to as large a constituency as the technology permits them to reach.

Diversity strategies of the 1990s are sophisticated initiatives designed to increase the numbers of women and minorities and other individuals from diverse backgrounds to help libraries and other organizations attract new customers, adapt to changing markets, and become more efficient. Managing diversity is a comprehensive process that begins with an assessment of an organization and its way of conducting business. The strategies based on this assessment focus on organizational and individual change. They are most successful when they are integrated into the strategic planning of the organization.

Managers are responsible for ensuring that employees at every level feel valued and positive about the workplace and the people with whom they work. At the same time, employees must be made to understand their role in ensuring that organizational objectives are met.

Diversity management can be defined as creating and maintaining an environment in which each person is respected because of his or her differences and where all can contribute and be rewarded on the basis of their accomplishments. Library managers more than ever are concerned with developing the potential of every employee. They must come up with new ways to identify high-potential employees, educate a culturally sensitive staff, and tap overlooked sources of dedicated employees.

Managing a diverse workforce means managing people who aren't like you and who don't necessarily aspire to be like you. Diversity encompasses the obvious and not-so-obvious differences. It's also about taking differences into account while developing a cohesive plan that unites people in a common pursuit. Diversity is not limited to questions about multicultural issues or gender, disabilities, or sexual orientation. Managers must also consider things such as age, work/family issues, economic status, education, religion, geographic origin, and position in the organization. Diversity includes everyone.

Basic Assumptions

To simplify our discussion we're going to assume that:

- Your organization has committed itself to introducing a diversity-management initiative and that this commitment is shown by a focus on continuous assessment, quality, and change.

- You believe in the importance and urgency of this effort and are willing to make a personal commitment to adjust your viewpoints and management methods to meet the needs of the organization.

- You are willing and prepared to invest the time and energy in making diversity strategies an integral part of your unit's business operations and the way you supervise.

While you may not be in a position to have an immediate effect on your organization's strategic planning process, there are a number of steps you can take to ensure that your unit is operating within a proactive mode.

- Create a safe, tolerant, and cooperative working environment to ensure maximum productivity. Encourage people to develop new skills and to take on new opportunities as they progress in the organization.

- Demonstrate in a way that is cost effective for the organization that every employee is equally valued. Recognize and respect opinions, practices, and behaviors of others.

- Give people guidance on acceptable and unacceptable work behaviors. Take action when you see a need to change the behavior of the people who work with you.

- Every time new people come into your work unit, ask yourself what is happening that will make them part of the team or exclude them from the team.

- Empower all employees to contribute their individual knowledge, talents, and skills fully to the organization.

- Set aside personal assumptions about individual work styles and personalities, and figure out how to use all ideas and talents.

- Be patient and flexible.

- Familiarize yourself with the laws and regulations governing employment discrimination, affirmative action, and the demographics of the labor pool and customers you serve.

- Examine and change policies, procedures, and practices that may be barriers to success for those who are different.

- Ensure that everyone understands the organization vision, mission, goals, and objectives.

- Ensure that all decisions are business decisions tied to the organization's plan.

- Eliminate obstacles that get in the way of any of these objectives.

Common Workplace Problems

When management neglects unresolved diversity issues in the workplace, the ability to achieve organizational goals is hampered. Some common problems to be on the lookout for are:

- Communication problems due to language or cultural barriers.
- Conflicts between and among employees that may undermine team cooperation and productivity.
- Anger and resentments that undermine both individual and group morale.
- Members of the team who sabotage the efforts of others deliberately or unconsciously.
- Demoralized individuals who may do just enough work to get by and collect a paycheck.
- Creativity and energy that disappear, inhibiting the group's growth and progress.

A group's failure to contribute effectively to the overall organization may affect the latter's competitive position in the marketplace and reflect negatively on the organization's ability to provide the level and quality of service required or expected.

Problem-Solving Strategies

Here are some—but not the only—ways to address problems once they have been identified:

- State your position on teamwork clearly: Teamwork means getting along with different people in the business environment in order to be productive and creative. This requires putting aside stereotypes and prejudices and avoiding personality conflicts.
- Set mutual goals with your employees for improving the unit's or organization's performance. Empower employees to follow through on these goals, setting up a reporting schedule to track their progress.

- State your expectations in terms of individual and group behavior in writing and distribute this document to all employees.
- Hold team meetings frequently. In follow-up meetings you and your employees can assess the team's progress toward its goals and make adjustments as needed.
- Help employees develop their abilities and skills through training and counseling.
- Emphasize that you will not tolerate discriminatory (e.g., sexist, ageist, or racist) language or behavior. Make it clear that any such language or behavior will be noted in your employees' performance appraisals.
- Counsel and, if necessary, discipline team members who continue to exhibit negative attitudes and behavior.
- Give employees continuing feedback on their progress and public recognition for their achievements. All employees need to contribute equally but not in the same way or at the same pace.
- Celebrate success, however small.

Personal Guidelines for Supervisors

Part of your responsibility as a supervisor is to model the behaviors that you expect from your employees. It is important that you be aware of your own attitude, stereotypes, and expectations and be open to discovering the limitations they place on your perspective.

- Don't let any incident pass without action. To do so sends the message that you agree with such behavior or attitudes. While intervention need not always take place at the exact time of the incident, it must be brought up at an appropriate time.
- Don't be afraid of possible tension or conflict; it may be unavoidable. There are deep-seated biases that won't change without some struggle.
- Recognize the long-term struggle: "ism's" won't be eradicated in a day; this is a process of change and growth.

• Remember that issues of human dignity, equality, and safety are nonnegotiable.

Outcomes of Managing Diversity

There are positive and measurable outcomes of integrating diversity strategies into your management practices. Among them are:

increased organizational effectiveness,

increased performance levels,

reduced conflict,

improved morale,

better teamwork,

greater cooperation,

fewer lawsuits,

improved recruitment and retention,

more effective job assignments and evaluations,

better client relations,

improved customer loyalty,

better access to facts,

better information,

improved problem solving.

Heterogeneous groups have been shown to outperform homogeneous groups on a wide range of measures.

Conclusion

Forward-thinking organizations recognize that managing diversity requires the kind of corporate culture that will attract and retain the best and the brightest staff and allow those employees to maximize their abilities and talents, ensuring that your organization is considered the best in its class.

There are no quick fixes for managing diversity. Managers are being challenged to identify and develop strategies and initiatives that are integral to improving work relationships and thus creating successful organizations. Tying diversity goals and objectives to the organization's mission makes good management sense. Libraries that move into the next century with a well-managed and diverse workforce will be better able to serve their widening universe of customers.

Suggested Reading

Bates, Tierney. "Making Quality Changes at SSA"(Interview with Social Security Administration Deputy Commissioner for Human Resources Ruth Pierce). *The Public Manager: The New Bureaucrat* 22 (Winter 1993): 55.

Baytos, Lawrence M. *Designing and Implementing Successful Diversity Programs.* Englewood Cliffs, N.J.: Prentice Hall, 1995.

Blank, Renee, and Sandra Slipp. *Voices of Diversity: Real People Talk about Problems and Solutions in a Workplace Where Everyone Is Not Alike.* New York: AMACON, American Management Association, 1994.

Buhler, Patricia. "Understanding Cultural Diversity and Its Benefits." (Managing in the '90s). *Supervision,* 54 (July 1993): 17.

Carnevale, Anthony Patrick. *The American Mosaic: An In-depth Report on the Future of Diversity at Work.* New York: McGraw-Hill, 1995.

Certo, Samuel C. *Modern Management: Diversity, Quality, Ethics, and the Global Environment.* 6th ed. Boston: Allyn and Bacon, 1994.

Crampton, Suzanne M., John W. Hodge, and Jaideep G. Motwani. "Diversity and Career Development Issues in the 90s." *Supervision,* 55 (June 1994): 6.

Crampton, Suzanne M., John W. Hodge, and Jaideep G. Motwani. "Relationship between Managing Diversity and Merit-based Systems." *Supervision,* 54 (June 1993): 17.

Fernandez, John P., and Mary Barr. *The Diversity Advantage: How American Business Can Out-perform Japanese and European Companies in the Global Marketplace.* New York: Lexington Books, 1993.

Fyock, Catherine D. *Cultural Diversity: Challenges and Opportunities,* Managing Diversity Series. Burr Ridge, Ill.: Irwin, 1994.

Gardenswartz, Lee, and Anita Rowe. *Managing Diversity: A Complete Desk Reference and Planning Guide.* Homewood, Ill.: Business One Irwin, 1993.

Griggs, Lews Brown, and Lente-Louise Louw, eds. *Valuing Diversity: New Tools for a New Reality.* New York: McGraw-Hill, 1995.

Jackson, Susan E., and Associates. *Diversity in the Workplace: Human Resources Initiatives,* The Professional Practice Series. New York: Guilford Press, 1992.

Loden, Marilyn, and Judy B. Rosener. *Workforce America!: Managing Employee Diversity As a Vital Resource.* Homewood, Ill.: Business One Irwin, 1991.

Plunkett, W. Richard. *Supervision: Diversity and Teams in the Workplace.* 8th ed. Upper Saddle River, N.J.: Prentice-Hall, 1995.

Pollar, Odette, and Rafael Gonzalez. *Dynamics of Diversity: Strategic Programs for Your Organization.* Menlo Park, Calif.: Crisp Publications, 1994.

Rasmussen, Tina. *The ASTD Trainer's Sourcebook,* ASTD Trainer's Sourcebook Series. New York: McGraw-Hill, 1996.

Riggs, Donald E., and Patricia A. Train, eds. *Cultural Diversity in Libraries.* New York: Neal-Schuman, 1994.

Steffey, Marda N. "Managing Diversity in the Classroom" (Training 101: Training in the Kaleidoscope). *Training & Development,* 47 (April 1993): 22.

Swift, Evangeline W. "Glass Ceilings and Equity" (Managing Diversity). *The Public Manager: The New Bureaucrat,* 21 (Winter 1992): 24.

Thomas, R. Roosevelt. *Beyond Race and Gender: Unleashing the Power of Your Total Work Force by Managing Diversity.* New York: AMACOM, American Management Association, 1991.

Trickett, Edison J., Roderick J. Watts, and Dina Berman, eds. *Human Diversity: Perspectives on People in Context,* Social and Behavioral Science Series. San Francisco: Jossey-Bass, 1994.

Walton, Sally J. *Cultural Diversity in the Workplace,* The Business Skills Express Series. Burr Ridge, Ill.: Irwin Professional Publications, 1994.

Zauderer, Donald G. "Reflections on Achieving Career Success" (Managing/Valuing Diversity). *The Public Manager: The New Bureaucrat,* 22 (Summer 1993): 56.

10

Conflict Resolution

Karen D. Jette

Circulation Librarian
Purdue University Library

C onflict is a fact of life in organizations. Conflict occurs when two or more people differ in their goals, the methods by which to achieve their goals, or their viewpoint. There is generally a problem underlying the conflict. A "problem" may be a change in the workplace, a change in the workload, a person's attitude toward his or her job, unresolved personal matters that a person carries to the workplace, dislike of an individual or his or her behavior at work, or a lack of respect for another person.

This chapter addresses conflict occurring between two or more staff members, between a supervisor and a staff member, between a supervisor and a peer, or between a supervisor and his or her superior.

Other sorts of conflict, which are not discussed here, are conflict between library patrons and staff or the library administration and an employee union. However, the same basic techniques may be useful for resolving these types of conflicts as well.

Conflict can be nonemotional or emotional. Nonemotional conflict is easier to deal with than emotional conflict because nonemotional conflict tends to be more rational and cerebral. The conflicting parties do not take their differences of opinions as a personal attack. In an emotionally charged conflict, the parties are likely to take the conflict as a personal indictment. In a conflict where emotions are involved, "each party wants to win (or worse, just defeat the other) regardless of whose solution is better. . . . Personal interests become more important than the interests of the organization."[1]

Sources of Conflict

Conflict has many causes, including: poor communication, changes in the workplace, clashes over scarce resources, material goals, hostile attitudes, aggressiveness, hatred, individual differences, interdepartmental relations, job ambiguity, deficiencies in the information system, environmental stress, need for control, and people who take an intensely personal interest in their job.

Problems start with behaviors and mind-sets. Differences of opinion may escalate into conflict. People's reaction to nonneutral language may end up causing conflict. Personal behaviors may cause conflict.

Radical change, such as newly automating a department, may lead to job insecurity for some people, causing a rift between "those who are comfortable with technology and those who are not. It may divide older staff from younger staff."[2] Downsizing or organizationwide changes that create fuzzy workplace boundaries may have a negative impact on staff and trigger problematic behavior in staff who are territorial and insecure.

Less dramatic changes may also lead to problems, as change may cause insecurity or edginess and lead people to speculate on how to protect their jobs. The change may be the arrival of a new employee, a new computer that everyone wants to use, the restructuring of an entire department, or giving an assignment to two or more people who then cannot agree on the direction the project should go, or have antithetical ideas about how to achieve the desired end. Other causes of conflict can be factionalism (failure to see the "big picture") or a person's behavior, attitude, or emotional response.

You may have generated the problem yourself. If you place unrealistic goals on your staff, *you* will not have a problem, but you have caused a problem for your staff. It is your staff who are under unrealistic pressure that you created. You may not feel that there are any problems until the project is due (unless someone complains to you in the meantime).

Sometimes people exhibit behaviors that cause conflict within the workplace. While these behaviors may help a person achieve his or her own agenda, they may cause problems for others in the unit. Some typical examples are:

- *Control addicts:* these people are territorial. They tend to refuse assistance from anyone else. Sometimes they never write anything down so that no one else knows how to perform the tasks that they perform. Control addicts who have other staff members working for them may have rules for everything. Everything has to be done their way, and they have to have the last word. These people are basically insecure.

- *Whiners:* these people complain about a great many things, from the petty to the truly important.

- *Bullies:* these people may like to start fights and intimidate others.

- *Know-it-alls:* these people have an opinion about everything. They hate to admit when they are wrong. They are often perceived as insensitive by others because they frequently have a brusque manner.

- *Brown-nosers:* these people may be highly competitive overachievers who just want your attention.

- *Cynics:* these people react negatively to new ideas and may have a wet-blanket effect on other staff.

- *Game players:* these people come in different types. One type likes to push other people's "hot buttons" in order to watch them react. Another, more insidious, type likes to play games of one-upmanship and games in which they win, you lose. This second type may seem to be a team player, but is not.

- *Difficult people,* who may have attributes of multiple behavior types listed above.

As a supervisor you need to separate the behaviors from the personalities of the people involved. Address the specific behavior that is causing a problem when trying to resolve conflicts in the unit. In a later section we will discuss ways of empowering your staff so that they are able to resolve issues among themselves, and won't need to call on you.

Internal conflict occurs when a person is confronted with a fact that he or she believed to be impossible. Internal conflict can also be caused by interpersonal confrontations. When a person disagrees with another to the extent that he or she experiences internal conflict, that person generally resorts to defensive behavior. The behavior such people exhibit depends on the depth and breadth of their experience. An empowered, mature person may be able to rise above the situation, cool off, and examine the problem from the point of view of the "big picture." People who are not empowered or are less secure may dig in and use defensive behaviors they learned from their parents and "sandbox" friends.

Other types of behaviors can also cause members of your unit to become defensive. A defensive response can lead to further conflict. We may behave defensively when we

fear that someone is passing judgment on us,

feel that someone is trying to manipulate or trick us,

feel as though we are ignored or unimportant,

are being talked down to and made to feel stupid or inadequate, or

feel that we cannot communicate with others.[3]

Put the Problem in Context

Conflict resolution begins with identifying the problem that underlies the conflict. Collect the facts. How has the problem escalated into conflict? Once you have identified the problem, examine its context. Is the problem one-to-one person, one-to-many, or many-many? If the problem is one "team" or "side" against the other, then you have a serious difficulty. Either the department is divided within itself, or there is an interdepartmental conflict.

Ask yourself "How long has the problem been going on? Is the problem symptomatic of a larger issue? What kind of conflict is it? What is the history of this problem?" If you are new to the job, you may want to get in touch with your predecessor or your supervisor to find out the history of the problem and the participants involved in the dispute.

If two people focus on making each other react, they will escalate the conflict and seldom or never confront the problem. Frequently when two or more people are in conflict with each other they are not focusing on the problem and when asked what the problem is, they are likely to reply "the other party." Confront the problem, not the person. If the problem stems from one person's behavior, focus on the behavior, not the person.

If it is obvious that one person is causing the problem, then it behooves the supervisor to speak to that person. However, do your homework before confronting him or her. Then make an appointment to see the person alone in your office or in some quiet place away from the other staff members and discuss the difficult behavior. Bring the problem to the staff member's attention. Provide objective performance data in order to prevent the appearance of a personal attack. Be clear about your expectations.

If no improvements are made and firing the employee is not an option, you may have to settle for long-term conflict resolution.

Confronting Problems

Do not let a conflict go on indefinitely, as this is bad for the entire department. Win/lose is not a good game for teams or organizations because it means that someone, maybe even a department, loses, resulting in a slowdown, waste of time and money, and low staff morale. If one department suffers, it is detrimental to the entire organization. If the entire organization is affected, no one stands to win in the long run. You want to play a win/win game that results in cooperation.

One goal in dealing with conflict should be attaining long-term stability. Once you know what the problem is, and what caused the problem in the first place, the solution often becomes self-evident (perhaps a change in procedures).[4] If the problem is a person's behavior, then you are going to have to insist that the person modify his or her behavior. You may also find it effective to modify the way you have been responding to that person.

Management Styles

As conflicts arise, analyze the situation and the individuals involved. It is important not to escalate the conflict by reacting prematurely. A hasty and poorly thought out response may be just what one party to the conflict is looking for in order to win. You want a win/win situation where both sides participate in solving the problem. Once you have developed a strategy for handling the conflict, stick to it.

There are six different conflict resolution styles that can be used by the manager.

1. *Avoidance/noninvolvement.* Basically, the supervisor pretends the conflict does not exist. This reaction may be an appropriate response if the cause of the conflict is beyond the supervisor's control or not of critical importance. Avoiding for the short term may also be used in the early stages of a conflict to buy time to collect the facts. However, this response to a conflict is unlikely to solve problems in the long run and may lead to passive or withdrawn behavior. When the conflict is between peers, avoidance may damage an important working relationship.

2. *Domineering.* Best used in emergencies; here the manager uses his or her rank over staff. This method is not recommended for the solution of long-term conflicts.

3. *Accommodation:* giving in.

4. *Compromise:* going part way. Here both parties to the conflict agree to give up something in order to reach a "mutually acceptable resolution."[5] This method may be used to resolve emotional conflict. As both parties must yield a little, neither is likely to feel the other party got a better deal.

5. *Collaboration:* joint problem solving. All the parties to the problem get together to reach a satisfactory solution. This approach is time-consuming but it has the advantage of moving the focus of the conflict from the emotional to the non-emotional.[6]

6. *Therapy:* counseling the person with the problem.

You can't change or avoid difficult people, but you can change the way you deal with them and the effect they have on you.

Negotiation and Mediation

Negotiation and mediation techniques are generally used to resolve difficult conflicts. You might use negotiation with a peer or a boss, or an employee union. You might possibly be called in to act as a third-party negotiator. Since a person generally becomes defensive in an emotionally charged confrontation, resolving the conflict requires that you place as much emotional distance as possible between yourself and the incident. As William Ury phrases it, "go to the balcony" and take a look at the big picture.[7] Wait until you've cooled off before resuming. Negotiation is usually an ongoing process, not a one-time effort. This is especially true if you mistake a symptom for the actual underlying problem.

As a supervisor you must assume the role of mediator when conflicting parties have reached an impasse. A mediator does not take sides but remains nonpartisan and does not become emotionally involved. Start the process by speaking to each party individually, then set up an appointment for both parties to speak with you present as mediator.

According to Dan DeStephen, the mediation process has six steps:[8]

1. Prepare the parties to mediate.
2. Listen to the problem from each individual's perspective.
3. Identify the issue or issues.
4. Generate solutions.
5. Generate an agreement.
6. Reinforce the agreement.

Attack the problem that underlies the difficulty. Do not attack the people involved. Everyone should be on the same side trying to resolve the problem.

When you reinforce the agreement, write the agreement down on paper and have both parties sign it. Both parties should get a copy of the written agreement.

When Conflict Resolution Doesn't Work

Sometimes you cannot reach a resolution. All that you can strive for is long-term stability, especially if you have a difficult person in your department whose behaviors do not warrant termination, or if you have constant change occurring in the department. Conflict management implies maintaining an equilibrium, not a permanent resolution.

Avoid Being a Party to Conflict

When someone sends you a memo or speaks to you and you want to react negatively, step aside mentally and think. Is this person pushing one of your "hot buttons"? Learn to react differently, underreact, or not to react immediately.

If you are a party to conflict, you may want to try collaborating or compromising. Donald Weiss lays out the following four-part method for taking action that you can use when confronting someone whose behavior has been causing a problem:[9]

1. Arrange a private meeting. Using nonthreatening terms, state the purpose of the meeting. Jointly accept responsibility for working on the problem by using "we" rather than "you" statements.
2. Exchange viewpoints. Hear the other person out first, then express your opinion. Let the other person offer a solution. If you agree with the offered solution, go to step 4. If not, go to step 3.
3. If you do not agree with the other party's offered solution, state your opinion clearly and succinctly. In order to resolve the disagreement, go back to step 2 and exchange viewpoints again.
4. Together, design an action plan for ending the problem. Set deadlines and progress review dates.

Empowering Your Staff

If you are the manager of a department whose staff are in conflict, develop a strategic goal of establishing long-term equilibrium within your department. It can be beneficial to examine the conflict within the context of the long-term goals of the department. You may find that in order to correct the conflict and establish long-term equilibrium, you need to introduce change in the work-place. Any changes in methods of handling conflict within your group should be discussed with staff well in advance of their implementation. Ask for your staff's input, so that the change is collaborative. Follow up with staff after the change has been implemented to see how they are coping with the agreed-upon process for handling conflict.

Empowered staff may have disagreements that will not escalate into conflict because they are able to reach a compromise. Teach your staff how to discuss conflicts and then if necessary to approach you with a problem and various solutions so that you may help them reach a solution. Communicate with them so that they have a better idea of the "big picture." Factions, i.e. groups of narrow minded people who "don't get the big picture," are often a major source of conflict. Discourage factional thinking. Encouraging thinking in terms of the whole organization should cut down on conflict.[10]

Make sure that your staff are aware that they can disagree without being disagreeable. A disagreement is different from a conflict because a disagreement involves a difference of opinion, belief, or idea, while a conflict rejects the other person's point of view as invalid. One may disagree without invalidating the other's point of view. A compromise can be reached by two parties who accept each other's point of view as valid.

Prepare your staff by communicating with them and if need be teaching them how to think through a problem. Develop guidelines for resolving conflicts before conflicts arise. Teach your staff conflict resolution and management skills.

Avoid being sidetracked onto tangential issues such as how decisions are made, or who had the right to give input and what issues are relevant. To ensure that the discussion does not get caught up in these tangential issues, the supervisor should develop rules or guidelines for handling conflict before conflicts arise. This should help keep the staff focused on the issue at hand.

Conclusion

As a supervisor, you can establish an atmosphere that will make it easier to cope with conflicts. Ideally, the best way to handle conflict is through prevention. These are several ways to avoid conflict in the organization:

- Provide an employee assistance program for staff. Consult with your organization's personnel office for more information about how an employee assistance program can help with conflict resolution.
- Help staff recognize that they share a common goal: that of making the organization successful.
- Develop an atmosphere in which contributions to the organizations are perceived as more important than anyone's personal status.
- Encourage candid and assertive communication between coworkers without asking them to confide too much.
- Distribute tips for handling conflict.
- Organize a workshop on conflict resolution.[11]
- Establish guidelines for resolving conflicts.

Notes

1. William Fisher and Glen Koue, "Conflict Management," *Library Administration and Management* 5 (1991): 145.
2. Ibid., 146.
3. Jaine Carter, "How to Handle Disagreement," *Management Solutions* 32 (September 1987): 30.
4. Donald Weiss, "How to Deal with Unpleasant People Problems," *Supervisory Management* 37 (March 1992): 1.
5. Fisher and Koue, op. cit., 148.
6. Ibid., 148.
7. William Ury, *Getting Past No: Negotiating Your Way from Confrontation to Cooperation,* rev. ed. (New York: Bantam Books, 1993), 31.
8. Dan DeStephen, "Mediating Those Office Conflicts," *Management Solutions* 33 (March 1988): 8–10.
9. Donald Weiss, "How to Handle Difficult People," *Management Solutions* 33 (February 1988): 38.
10. Fisher and Koue, op. cit., 148.

11. Andrew E. Schwartz, "How to Handle Conflict between Employees," *Supervisory Management* 37 (June 1992): 9.

Suggested Reading

Birdsall, William. "The Library Manager as Therapist." *The Journal of Academic Librarianship* 16 (July 1990): 209–12.

Carbone, Joe. "Keeping Peace on the Job." *Supervisory Management* 37 (December 1992): 3.

Carson, Paula Phillips, Kerry David Carson, and Joyce Shouest Phillips. *The Library Manager's Deskbook: 102 Expert Solutions to 101 Common Dilemmas.* Chicago: American Library Association, 1995.

Carter, Jaine. "How to Handle Disagreement." *Management Solutions* 32 (Sept. 1987): 27–33.

Carter, Janet Houser. "How to Cope with Angry Employees or Colleagues." *Supervisory Management* 36 (April 1991): 6–7.

Collison, William. *Conflict Reduction: Turning Conflict to Cooperation.* Dubuque, Iowa: Kendall/Hunt, 1988.

DeStephen, Dan. "Mediating Those Office Conflicts." *Management Solutions* 33 (March 1988): 4–10.

Fisher, William, and Glen Koue. "Conflict Management." *Library Administration and Management* 5 (Summer 1991): 145–50.

Jones, Katina Z. *Succeeding with Difficult People.* Stamford, Conn.: Longmeadow Press, 1992.

Kathman, Jane McGurn, and Michael D. Kathman. "Conflict Management in the Academic Library." *The Journal of Academic Librarianship* (May 1990): 145–49.

Premeaux, Shane R., and R. Wayne Mondy. "Problem Employees: The Cynic." *Management Solutions* 31 (October 1986): 14–16.

Schwartz, Andrew E. "How to Handle Conflict between Employees." *Supervisory Management* 37 (June 1992): 9.

Sharplin, Arthur, R. Wayne Mondy, and Shane R. Premeaux. "Resolving Employee Conflict." *Supervision* 48 (June 1986): 3–6.

Sheppard, I. Thomas. "Managing Those You Don't Like." *Management Solutions* 32 (September 1987): 34–36.

Straub, Joseph T. "Dealing with Complainers, Whiners, and General Malcontents." *Supervisory Management* 37 (July 1992): 1–2.

Ury, William. *Getting Past No: Negotiating Your Way from Confrontation to Cooperation.* Revised edition. New York: Bantam Books, 1993.

Weiss, Donald H. "How to Deal with Unpleasant People Problems." *Supervisory Management* 37 (March 1992): 1–2.

_____. "How to Handle Difficult People." *Management Solutions* 33 (February 1988): 33–38.

_____. "Mediating between Warring Employees." *Supervisory Management* 38 (December 1993): 3.

Wilcox, James R., Ethel M. Wilcox, and Karen M. Cowan. "Communicating Creatively in Conflict Situations." *Management Solutions* 31 (October 1986): 18–24.

Index

J oan Giesecke is the Dean of Libraries, University of Nebraska–Lincoln Libraries. She has received a doctorate in public administration from George Mason University, an MLS from the University of Maryland, a master's degree in management from Central Michigan University, and a BA in economics from SUNY at Buffalo. Giesecke's research interests include organizational decision-making and management skills. She has developed a training program for managers and has presented a variety of papers on management and supervisory skills. She is a former editor of *Library Administration and Management* and has published numerous articles on management issues.